D1882556

MEMOIRS
OF
THE EMPEROR JAHANGUEIR

MEMOIRS
OF
THE EMPEROR JAHANGUEIR

TRANSLATED FROM A PERSIAN MANUSCRIPT,
BY
DAVID PRICE

GYAN

Published by

Gyan Publishing House
5, Ansari Road
Daryaganj, New Delhi-110002
Phone: 011-47034999, 9811692060
E-mail: books@gyanbooks.com

Distribution Network
gyanbooks.com
India, USA, Canada, UK, Australia, France

© Publisher

All rights reserved. No part of this work may be reproduced, stored, adapted, or transmitted in any form or by any means, electronic, mechanical, photocopying, micro-filming, recording or otherwise, or translated in any language, without the prior written permission of the copyright owner and the publisher.

ISBN: 978-81-212-8356-4 (PB)
First Published, 1829

2nd Impression 2023

Printed at: Gyan Press, Delhi.

The book is sold subject to the condition that it shall not, by way of trade or otherwise, be lent, resold, hired out, or otherwise circulated without the prior publisher's written consent.

MEMOIRS OF THE EMPEROR JAHANGUEIR
TRANSLATOR: DAVID PRICE

MEMOIRS

OF

THE EMPEROR JAHANGUEIR,

WRITTEN BY HIMSELF;

AND

TRANSLATED FROM A PERSIAN MANUSCRIPT,

BY

MAJOR DAVID PRICE,

Of the Bombay Army; Member of the Royal Asiatic Society of Great Britain and Ireland; of the Oriental Translation Committee; and of the Royal Society of Literature.

LONDON:

PRINTED FOR THE ORIENTAL TRANSLATION COMMITTEE,

AND SOLD BY

J. MURRAY, ALBEMARLE STREET; PARBURY, ALLEN, & CO., LEADENHALL STREET;

AND HOWELL & STEWART, HOLBORN.

1829.

ADVERTISEMENT.

The Persian Manuscript which has furnished materials for this Work not being distinguished by any particular title, the Translator would have ventured to style it the واقعات جهانگیری WAKIAATI JAHANGUIRI, or to bestow on it some other name equally signifying "Incidents in "the Reign of the Emperor Jahangueir." But to supply an Oriental name from mere conjecture seemed unnecessary, as the contents could be indicated with sufficient accuracy in an English title-page.

Besides, from some extracts, occupying about seventeen pages in the "Asiatick Miscellany" (printed at Calcutta 1785-1786, vol. ii., pp. 71-173) it would appear to be the same, or nearly the same, with that work which was described by an accomplished Orientalist, who translated those passages (James Anderson, Esq.) as the "Toozuk e "Jehangeery (تزوک جهانگیری), or Memoirs of Jehangeer written by "himself, and containing a History of the Transactions of the First "thirteen years of his Reign." But Mr. Anderson did not profess to give more than a few extracts from the Toozuk; and a comparison of these with the present work, will show that he must have occasionally omitted whole pages between certain facts recorded in both.

N.B. In this work the Arabic or Persian letter خ is expressed by *kh*, as in *Khaun, Sheikh,* &c. The letter ج in the beginning of a word is generally expressed by *J*, as in *Jummaudy, Jaguir;* in other parts of a word by *dj*, as *Hidjerah, Adjmeir,* or by the simple *j*, as in *Punjaub, Khanjar,* &c. The letter غ is represented by *gh*, as *Chirâgh, Afghan:* the Arabic ث by *th*, as in *Thauni:* the long ا generally by *au*, as in *Khaun, Zauhed, Bauz,* &c. The ي at the beginning of a word by *Y*, as in *Yaheya;* in other parts generally by *ei*, as *Peishkesh, Seleim, Parveiz,* &c. At the beginning of a word و is expressed by *V*, as in *Vezzeir;* in other places by *w*, as *Diwan;* or by *ou*, as in *Roum, Nour,* &c. To express the Persian letter گ before ي *guei* or *gui* are used, as in *Jahangueir, Jaguir,* &c.

AUTOBIOGRAPHICAL MEMOIRS

OF THE

REIGN OF THE EMPEROR JAHANGUEIR.

To HIM whose name is inscribed at the head of all that has existence; the characters of whose glory are stamped on the walls and portals of the universe: to the Eternal Designer, who with a word, from the bosom of nothing, brought forth the celestial spheres and the elements of created nature: to the Omnipotent Architect, who spread above us the alternate vaults of the firmament, and arrayed this globe of earth with the splendours of his might: to Him be endless praise and illimitable gratitude; and on our prophet Mahommed, that most excellent of created beings, who released mankind from the mazes of error, and conducted them to the high road of truth and duty, be countless blessings: to whom was given, from God, authority over all terrestrial power, and over all other prophets the pre-eminence; the Messiah himself bearing the glad tidings of his approach; of his approach at whose lamp the great legislator of Israel, the God-spoken prophet, sought to secure a spark of heavenly light.

For a memorial of sundry events incidental to myself, I have undertaken to describe a small portion, in order that some traces thereof may be preserved on the records of time.

On Thursday, then, the eighth of the latter month of Jummaudy, of the year of the Hidjera one thousand and fourteen,* at the metropolis of Agrah, and in the forenoon of the day, being then arrived at the age of thirty-eight, I became Emperor, and under auspices the most felicitous, took my seat on the throne of my wishes. Let it not produce a smile that I should have set my heart on the delusions of this world. Am I greater than Solomon, who placed his pillow

upon

* Corresponding with the 10th of October, A.D. 1605. According to some authorities, the Emperor Akbar died on Wednesday the 10th of the latter Jummaudy, A.H. 1014, corresponding with the 12th of October, A.D. 1605; which would make the accession of Jahangueir to have preceded the death of his father by two days.

upon the winds? As at the very instant that I seated myself on the throne the sun rose from the horizon, I accepted this as the omen of victory, and as indicating a reign of unvarying prosperity. Hence I assumed the titles of Jahangueir Padshah, and Jahangueir Shah: the world-subduing emperor; the world-subduing king. I ordained that the following legend should be stamped on the coinage of the empire: "Stricken at Agrah by that Khossrou, the safeguard of the world; the sovereign splendour of the faith, Jahangueir, son of the imperial Akbar."

On this occasion I made use of the throne prepared by my father, and enriched at an expense without parallel, for the celebration of the festival of the new year, at the entrance of the sun into Aries. In the fabrication of the throne a sum not far short of ten krours of ashrefies,* of five mithkals the ashrefy, was expended in jewels alone; a krour being the term for an hundred laks, and a lak being one hundred thousand, independently of three hundred maunns of gold, Hindustanny measure, employed in the workmanship, each maunn of Hind being equal to ten maunns of Irâk.† For the convenience of removal from place to place the throne was, moreover, so constructed, that it could be easily taken to pieces, and again put together at pleasure. The legs and body of the throne were at the same time loaded with fifty maunns of ambergris, so that wherever it might be found expedient to put it together, no further perfumes were necessary, for an assemblage of whatever magnitude.

Having thus seated myself on the throne of my expectations and wishes, I caused also the imperial crown, which my father had caused to be made after the manner of that which was worn by the great kings of Persia, to be brought before me, and then, in the presence of the whole assembled Ameirs, having placed it on my brows, as an omen auspicious to the stability and happiness of my reign, kept it there for the space of a full astronomical hour. On each of the twelve points of this crown was a single diamond of the value of one lak of ashrefies of five mithkals, the whole purchased by my father with the resources of his own government, not from any thing accruing to him by inheritance from his

* A krour of ashrefies is synonimous with gold mohrs, which I have reason to think would be equal to fifteen krours of rupees; and ten krours of ashrefies would be one hundred and fifty krours of rupees, or about one hundred and fifty millions sterling! an incredible sum. Instead therefore of ten, we shall read two krours of ashrefies, and thirty krours of rupees, still making thirty millions sterling. We shall here remark that *noble* would be the appropriate English version of ashrefy. Again, the Bombay maunn is estimated at about twenty-eight pounds, or a quarter of a hundred-weight; and three hundred maunns will therefore be about four tons of gold.

† Calculating the ashrefy as before, at fifteen rupees, this would make the value of each diamond £150,000 sterling, which multiplied by twelve will give the enormous sum of £1,800,000.

his predecessors. At the point in the centre of the top part of the crown was a single pearl of four mithkals, of the value of one lak of ashrefies; and on different parts of the same were set altogether two hundred rubies of one mithkal each, and each of the value of six thousand rupees.*

For forty days and forty nights I caused the nuggaurah, or great imperial state drum, to strike up, without ceasing, the strains of joy and triumph; and for an extent of nearly fifty zereibs around my throne, the ground was spread by my directions with the most costly brocades and gold embroidered carpets. Censors of gold and silver were disposed in different directions for the purpose of burning odoriferous drugs, and nearly three thousand camphorated wax lights, three cubits in length, in branches of gold and silver perfumed with ambergris, illuminated the scene from night till morning. Numbers of blooming youths, beautiful as young Joseph in the pavilions of Egypt, clad in dresses of the most costly materials, woven in silk and gold, with zones and amulets sparkling with the lustre of the diamond, the emerald, the sapphire, and the ruby, awaited my commands, rank after rank, and in attitude most respectful. And finally, the Ameirs of the empire, from the captain of five hundred to the commander of five thousand horse, and to the number of nine individuals, covered from head to foot in gold and jewels, and shoulder to shoulder, stood round in brilliant array, also waiting for the commands of their sovereign. For forty days and forty nights did I keep open to the world these scenes of festivity and splendour, furnishing altogether an example of imperial magnificence seldom paralleled in this stage of earthly existence.

Until he had attained to the age of eight and twenty my father had had no child that survived its birth beyond one astronomical hour; and the circumstance was to him the subject of very deep concern. To obtain, therefore, the object of his wishes in this respect, many and anxious were the supplications which he addressed to the throne of Omnipotence. While he languished in this state of anxiety, one of his Ameirs, aware of his unbounded reverence for, and confidence in the influence of the class of derveishes, mentioned to him one day, that at the tomb of the venerated Moyen-ud-dein Tehousty, at Adjmeir, there resided a peir, or holy recluse, distinguished for the purity of his life and manners, in which, as he said, not only in India, but in the whole world, he was that day without his equal. In the ardour of zeal and hope, my father expressed a determination, that should Providence bestow upon him a child that might survive, he would walk all the way on foot from the metropolis of Agrah to Adjmeir,

* Altogether, then, this superb symbol of supreme power may be valued at two millions and seventy thousand pounds sterling.

Adjmeir, a distance of not less than one hundred and forty kôss,* for the sole purpose of offering his vows at the shrine of the saint. As my father's determination sprung from the sincerity of his heart, just six months after the death of my last departed infant brother, namely, on Wednesday the seventeenth of the former month of Rebbeia, of the year of the Hidjerah 978,† the sun being in the twenty-fourth degree of *Libra*, and when seven gurrics of the day were passed, the Most High ushered the humble narrator of these events into this stage of existence.

Faithful to his engagement, my father, whose mansion is now on the empyrean, accompanied by several of the most distinguished Ameirs of his court, took his departure from Agrah, and proceeding on foot at the rate of five koss a day, presented himself on his arrival at Adjmeir before the shrine of Moyen-ud-dein, and having performed his devotions, hastened without further delay in quest of the derveish, through the influence of whose piety he had obtained the object of his anxious supplications. The pious recluse bore the name of Sheikh Seleim, and my father, on repairing to the place of his residence, then lodging me in his arms, intreated him to pray to God for the safety of his infant child. This however was not all: during his visit my father ventured to inquire of the derveish if he could undertake to tell him the number of the sons whom the Almighty in his providence had decreed to bestow upon him. Elated at the moment by the presence of his imperial visitor, the derveish did not hesitate to announce to my father that Providence would bless him with three sons. "Of these," cried my father, "I have cast the first-born into thy bosom."—"Blessings upon it," replied the derveish, "since thou hast committed the child to my arms, I have given him the name of Mahommed Seleim." Accepting these testimonies of attention on the part of the derveish as greatly auspicious to his hopes, my father then returned to his capital, where, for the space of fourteen years afterwards, he continued to maintain with this holy recluse an intercourse of the closest intimacy.

[In this place there appears something of an omission in the manuscript, as the imperial memorialist is made to refer rather abruptly to the village of Sikry, to which, in commemoration of the conquest of Gûjerat, he states that his father gave the name of Futtahpour—Nicopolis.]

I must however observe, continues the imperial narrator, that from my father's anointed lips, I never on any occasion heard myself called by the name of Mahommed Seleim; baba (child) being the more paternal and affectionate appellation

* The kôss is an indefinite measurement, from one and a half to two miles and upwards.

† 18th of August, A.D. 1570; this prince at his accession could therefore be no more than thirty-six.

lation by which he invariably addressed me. And, peradventure, I might have been contented to the last with the title of Sultan Seleim: but to place myself on a par with the monarchs of the Turkish empire (Roum), and considering that universal conquest is the peculiar vocation of sovereign princes, I thought it incumbent on me to assume at my accession that of Jahangueir Padshah, as the title which best suited my character: and I trust, with the aid of a gracious Providence, with length of life, and a favouring star, that I shall so acquit myself as to justify the appellation.

The very first ordinance which issued from me, on ascending the throne of my ancestors, was that which related to the chain of justice, one end of which I caused to be fastened to the battlements of the royal tower of the castle of Agrah, and the other to a stone pillar near the bed of the river Jumnah; to the end that, when at any time the dispensers of law under my authority might fail in the administration of justice, the injured party by applying his hand to the chain would find himself in the way of obtaining speedy redress. The chain was of gold, one hundred and forty guzz in length, with eighty small bells attached at different distances, and it was of the weight of sixty maunns of Hindûstaun, equal to six hundred maunns of Irâk.*

I instituted twelve special regulations, to be applied by the different functionaries of the empire as rules of conduct, never to be deviated from in their respective stations.

1. I remitted altogether to my subjects three several sources of revenue, the Zekhaut, Sermohary, and Tumgha, which in the whole yielded to my father no less than sixteen hundred Hindustany maunns of gold, equal to sixteen thousand maunns of Irâk.†

2. I ordained that wherever the property of God's people entrusted to my charge should be wrested from them, either by highway robbery or any other act of violence, the inhabitants of the district, as best knowing whence it proceeded, should be compelled to produce either the property or the depredator. I directed, when the district lay waste or destitute of inhabitants, that towns should be built, and the population registered, and every method resorted to that might contribute to protect the subject from injury. I charged the Jaguirdaurs, or feudatories of the empire, in such deserted places to erect mosques and substantial serrais, or stations for the accommodation of travellers, in order to render the district once more an inhabited country, and that wayfaring men might again be able to pass and repass in safety. For these purposes I provided

* About fifteen hundred-weight, reckoning the maunn at 28 lbs. or a quarter of an hundred-weight.

† About twenty-two tons and a half.

vided that where the district was immediately dependent on the crown, and the residence of a Kroury,* that officer was authorized to prosecute these works at the expense of the imperial treasury.

3. Merchants travelling through the country were not to have their bales or packages of any kind opened without their consent. But when they were perfectly willing to dispose of any article of merchandize purchasers were permitted to deal with them, without, however, offering any species of molestation.

4. When a person shall die and leave children, the individual not being in the employment of the state, no man whatever was to interfere a pin's point in his property, nor to offer the slightest molestation to the children: but when there were neither children nor direct or unquestionable heirs, the inheritance was to be applied to defray the expenses incurred for mosques and talaub, or water-tanks, so as to secure perpetual blessings on the soul of the departed.

5. No person was permitted either to make or sell either wine or any other kind of intoxicating liquor. I undertook to institute this regulation, although it is sufficiently notorious that I have myself the strongest inclination for wine, in which from the age of sixteen I have liberally indulged. And in very truth, encompassed as I was with youthful associates of congenial minds, breathing the air of a delicious climate—ranging through lofty and splendid saloons, every part of which decorated with all the graces of painting and sculpture, and the floors bespread with the richest carpets of silk and gold, would it not have been a species of folly to have rejected the aid of an exhilarating cordial—and what cordial can surpass the juice of the grape? May it not happen that theriauk, or opiates, or stimulants, have been rendered habitual to the constitution? and heaven forbid that this should deprive a man of the most generous feelings of his nature. With some acknowledged beneficial effects, it must however be confessed, that these indulgences to excess must expose a man's infirmities, prostrate his constitutional vigour, and awaken false desires, such being the most injurious properties belonging to the list of stimulants.† At the same time, we cannot but remember that kelourica is brother's son to theriauk.

For myself, I cannot but acknowledge that such was the excess to which I had carried my indulgence, that my usual daily allowance extended to twenty, and sometimes to more than twenty cups, each cup containing half a seir (about six

* This was an office instituted by Akbar, and the functionary was so called because he had the collection of a krour, or one hundred lak, of *daums*, of which latter there were forty to the rupee.

† The passage included in this paragraph has been so carelessly copied in the Persian manuscript, that we have had the greatest difficulty in making out the sense.

six ounces), and eight cups being equal to a maunn of Irâk.* So far, indeed, was this baneful propensity carried, that if I were but an hour without my beverage, my hands began to shake and I was unable to sit at rest. Convinced by these symptoms, that if the habit gained upon me in this proportion my situation must soon become one of the utmost peril, I felt it full time to devise some expedient to abate the evil: and in six months I accordingly succeeded in reducing my quantity gradually from twenty to five cups a day. At entertainments I continued, however, to indulge in a cup or two more: and on most occasions I made it a rule never to commence my indulgence until about two hours before the close of the day. But now that the affairs of the empire demand my utmost vigilance and attention, my potations do not commence until after the hour of evening prayer, my quantity never exceeding five cups on any occasion; neither would more than that quantity suit the state of my stomach. Once a day I take my regular meal, and once a day seems quite sufficient to assuage my appetite for wine; but as drink seems not less necessary than meat for the sustenance of man, it appears very difficult, if not impossible, for me to discontinue altogether the use of wine. Nevertheless, I bear in mind, and I trust in heaven that, like my grandfather Homayun, who succeeded in divesting himself of the habit before he attained to the age of forty-five, I also may be supported in my resolution, some time or other to abandon the pernicious practice altogether. " In a point wherein God has pronounced his sure displeasure, let the creature exert himself ever so little towards amendment, and it may prove, in no small degree, the means of eternal salvation."

6. No person was permitted to take up his abode obtrusively in the dwelling of any subject of my realm. On the contrary, when individuals serving in the armies of the state came to any town, and could without compulsion secure an abode by rent, it were commendable; otherwise they were to pitch their tents without the place, and prepare habitations for themselves. For what grievance could be more irksome to the subject than to see a perfect stranger obtrude into the bosom of his family, and take possession most probably of the most convenient part of his dwelling, leaving to his women and children, peradventure, not space enough to stretch out an arm!

7. No person was to suffer, for any offence, the loss of a *nose* or *ear*. If the crime were theft, the offender was to be scourged with thorns, or deterred from further transgression by an attestation on the Korân.†

8. The Krouries and Jaguirdaurs were prohibited from possessing themselves by

* About three pounds.

† The same defect in the manuscript already complained of, compels us here, as well as in several other places, to rely upon conjecture.

by violence of the lands of the subject, or from cultivating them on their own account; neither was the Jaguirdaur or feudatory of any district to exercise any sort of authority beyond the limits of his own, nor to force either man or beast from another district into his own. On the contrary, his attention was to be wholly and exclusively devoted to the cultivation and improvement of the district allotted to himself.

9. [This article is perfectly unintelligible in the manuscript, but seems directed to impose some restraint on the improper use of theriauk or antidotes of any kind, or possibly prescribing the rule by which they shall be administered.]

10. The governors in all the principal cities were directed to establish infirmaries or hospitals, with competent medical aid for the relief of the sick, who were to be conveyed thither; the expense to be defrayed from the imperial exchequer until the final recovery of the patient, who was then to be discharged with a sufficient sum of money for his exigencies.

11. During the month of my birth, which was that of the former Rebbeia, the use of all animal food was prohibited both in town and country; and at equidistant periods throughout the year a day was set apart, on which all slaughtering of animals was strictly forbidden. In every week also, on Thursday, that being the day of my accession, and Sunday, was forbidden the use of animal food, it being considered unjustifiable to deprive any animal of life on that day on which the creation of the world was finished. For a period of more than eleven years was the same abstinence observed by my father, during which on no consideration would he permit himself to taste of animal food on a Sunday. On that day, therefore, I thought it right to prohibit the use of such food in every place throughout my dominions.

12. I issued a decree confirming the dignitaries and feudatories of my father's government in all that they had enjoyed while he was living; and where I found sufficient merit, I conferred an advance of rank in various gradations. Thus a commander of ten horse I advanced to the command of fifteen, and so on in proportion to the highest dignitaries of the realm.

On this point I cannot restrain myself from invoking the judgment of heaven upon those unworthy servants who had not the understanding to appreciate the value of the benefits thus liberally bestowed upon them. Such, I am compelled to observe, is the perverseness of human nature, that there were among them individuals who could not be brought, without the greatest reluctance, to yield to me the ordinary marks of homage and allegiance.* With men thus turbulently

* Kornesh and tessleim. These remarks refer to the adherents of his eldest son Khossrou, of whom hereafter.

lently disposed, we ought not, I say, to negociate on any terms, because their views invariably tend towards convulsions on the state, and their increasing prayers are for dissention and civil broil, as offering the only means of advancing their own base and sordid plans of ambition, *forgetting that they are themselves the very description of men to be first swept away by the storm.*

So just was the observation ascribed to Shah Tahmasp of Persia, now in Paradise, that I cannot forbear to introduce it in this place. Having just finished a tank or reservoir near one of his palaces, it occurred to him to ask his courtiers what they thought the best substance with which to fill it, independently of water. One of them gave his opinion in favour of gold. "Thou hast well said," replied the monarch, "for thy prevailing propensity is avarice." Another said he should like to see it brimful of sherbet, sugar, and rose-water, intermingled with pieces of ice. "Apparently," observed the king, "thou art an opium-eater, and hast very correctly indicated thine appetite." Others described one thing, and others different sorts of things, according to their several ideas: but Shah Tahmasp concluded by a declaration, that neither of these opinions coincided with the sentiments of his own mind; for that, in his judgment, the reservoir could not be better filled than with the blood of turbulent and disaffected men, the agents of tumult and commotion.* And most truly, do I say, was it spoken; for since the death of my father, I have had abundant experience that the number of loyal and faithful men is deplorably small, and, if indeed at all to be met with, not more than one in a hundred thousand.

Of Shah Abbas, while I was yet prince royal, I remember hearing it related, that his attachment to Ferhaâd Khaun, one of his ministers, was so powerful, that once, when the minister lay sick of his wounds, his sovereign, during his frequent visits in the morning, was accustomed with his own tongue to lick the wounds; and he had been raised by his master to the very highest dignities in the Persian empire. Yet after all, was the monarch compelled to take off the head of the man so singularly cherished. I cannot entertain a doubt but that the Shah had too many reasons in justification: for long have I been convinced, that to tie up the hand against punishing the ingratitude of the traitor, is of all follies the most egregious. And yet, when thoroughly tried, the good and faithful servant cannot be too highly and liberally cherished. It cannot, however, be too often repeated, that the wretch who traffics for an advance of stipend at the moment his services are required, needs no further trial. He can be no other than a disloyal profligate.

* If the word in the manuscript be *keliktchee*, it would signify agents of commotion.

To the individual stipendiaries of the government I assigned, at the same time, an increased allowance, in the proportion of fifteen to ten (that is, to him that had only ten, I assigned fifteen rupees), and to novices in trade, artisans possibly employed in the different arsenals, from ten to twelve in the aggregate. I augmented the allowance to the inmates of my father's harram, consisting of nearly seven thousand individuals, from two to four ashrefies of five methkals a day each respectively,* and independently of the royal presents which I conveyed to them on the usual annual festivals and days of rejoicing. During the reign of my father, the ministers of religion and students in law and literature, to the number of two and three thousand, in the principal cities of the empire, were already allowed pensions from the state; and to these, in conformity with the regulations established by my father, I directed Meiran Sudder Jahzan, one of the noblest among the Seyeds of Herât, to allot a subsistence corresponding with their situation; and this not only to the subjects of my own realms, but to foreigners—to natives of Persia, Roum, Bokhára, and Azerbaijan, with strict charge that this class of men should not be permitted either want or inconvenience in any shape: "Wealth is from God—all power is from him—and these are his servants:"—and since it hath pleased him, from among so many hundred thousand laks of the human race, to chuse me for the monarch of a mighty empire, of which the reins have thus been placed in my hands, I could not be justified in permitting distress to lay hold of those devoted to his service, or in neglecting to make myself acquainted with all their wants, and to adopt them as the objects of my peculiar care. For how fearful my responsibility on the great and awful day of account, were my conduct to be the reverse of what is here stated.

In the next place I decreed a general pardon and enlargement of prisoners throughout the empire, so that from the fortress of Gualiar alone there were set at liberty not less than seven thousand individuals, some of whom had been in confinement for forty years. Of the number discharged altogether on this occasion, some conception may be formed when it is mentioned, that within the limits of Hindustan there are not less than two thousand four hundred fortresses of name and competent strength, exclusively of those in the kingdom of Bengal, which surpass all reckoning: for Rajah Maun Sing had not less than two hundred and eighty sons, all of whom, at one time or another, were in rebellion

* Calculating the ashrefy at fifteen rupees, this would make a daily expenditure, on this head alone, of £42,000, or £1,260,000 a month, and £15,120,000 per annum: a sum rather beyond credibility.

rebellion against the authority of their father; in the course of which, retiring to the summits of the hills, they there erected these forts to screen themselves from the punishment due to their parricidal rebellion. And yet will it be believed, that in the space of not more than four years, the whole of that country, a country of many months' journey in extent, with all its numberless forts, was completely subjugated by my father, all the sons of the Rajah being alternately destroyed; and the Rajah himself falling alive into the hands of his adversaries, finally submitted to the conqueror.

Among these my earliest regulations, I ordained that the precious metals included in the royalties of the empire should be coined anew in my own imperial name, assigning to each coin an altered denomination: thus, to the gold moher of two thousand tolahs,* I gave the name of nour-e-shahy—light of the kingdom; to that of one thousand tolahs, nour-jahaun—light of the world; to that of five hundred tolahs, nour-e-doulut—light of the state; to that of one hundred, nour-moher—light of the sun; and to that of one tolah, which was substituted for the gold rupee, I gave the designation of Nour-ud-deen Mahommed, Jahangueir Padshah—light of the faith of Mahommed, Jahangueir emperor. Moreover, for every one of these coins in gold I struck a corresponding piece in silver, exhibiting on one side the year of my reign, on the other the attestation of our faith: La-illauh-il-ullah, and Mahommed-ur-russoul-ullah—there is no God but God, and Mahommed is the messenger of God.

The city of Agrah, it were almost superfluous to observe, is one of the greatest in Hindustan; and being defended by a citadel of great antiquity, my father had caused such citadel to be thrown down, and a new fabric of hewn stone to be erected on the site, as will be noticed in another place. I shall here only remark further, that the city is built on both banks of the river Jumnah, that part which is situated on the hither, or western side, being four kôsse in breadth and ten kôsse in circumference, and that on the opposite side being not more than two kôsse in breadth, and three kôsse in circumference. The multiplicity of noble structures erected on all sides, such as mosques of superior magnitude, baths, spacious caravanserais, and splendid private palaces, are to an extent that would place it on a par with the most celebrated cities in Irâk, Khorassaun, and the famed territory beyond the Jeyhoun (the Oæure), the ordinary dwellings of the inhabitants being built, for the greater part, three

and

* As far as I can remember, on the western side of India the silver rupee was the weight of a tolah; and in Richardson's Persian Dictionary, under the word *sikkah*, the reader will find the description of a gold coin of the value of £300. The weight of two thousand rupees would however be preposterous for any portable coin; it must then have been of that value only, which would be about £200.

and four stories high. Such is the immensity of the population, that from the hour of evening prayer to the close of the first quarter of the night, the throng is so densely wedged, that it is not without the utmost difficulty the people can pass and repass along the streets.

As an attempt to ascertain in some degree the extent of this multitudinous population, I directed Melek Ally, the kotwaal, a superintendant of police, one day to make a tour through the city, and count the individuals assembled in the different maarekahs, or theatres for athletæ or pugilists; and his report was, that in none of these places did he find assembled less than two and three thousand persons, although it was neither the first of the new year, nor any of those days of public rejoicing on which it was usual for the people to appear abroad for amusement. From this it is considered that some estimate may be formed of the enormous multitude which thronged the city in every quarter. Add to this, that every day through the year there were conveyed to the place by boats along the Jumnah not less than ten thousand loads of fuel, and yet for dirrems it would be difficult to purchase a single branch, so rapid was the demand. For nearly eight months, moreover, which is the duration of the dry season, or the interval between the periodical rains, not less than five and six thousand horses for sale daily enter the city from Kabûl and the countries in that direction; and such is the rapidity with which they are disposed of, that not one is to be purchased on the succeeding day. In short, I do not know in the whole world, in magnitude and the multitude of its inhabitants, there is any city to be compared with the metropolis of Agrah.

With regard to situation, it lies in the second of the seven climates, with Kanouje to the east, Nagour to the west, Sumbul to the north, and to the south Chandeiry. [The imperial narrator introduces here the verses composed by Karuffy, a poet of Shirauz, in praise of Agrah, in the time of Akbar, when speaking of the palace of Sultan Khorrom, afterwards the Emperor Shahjahaun: which it is quite unnecessary. as well as tedious, to repeat.]

Agrah was, however, a city of considerable magnitude, even prior to the supremacy of the Afghans, and it is spoken of in terms of admiration by a poet of Gheznîn, in the time of Mûssaoud, the son of Ibrahim, the twelfth of the race of Sebectegîn, Mahmoud Ghazi being the fourth. With regard to the river Jumnah, we learn from the writings of the Hindûs, that it has its source in these mountains, which, from the intensity of the cold, are inaccessible to the approach of man without the greatest difficulty. When it first makes its appearance near Hasserabad to the north-west, it rushes with such impetuous force, that an elephant would be swept away like a straw. From the foot of the citadel of Agrah it bends its course in the direction of Bengal.

Again,

Again, when Sekunder Lodi was on his march from Dehly, which was at that period the metropolis of the Indian monarchy, for his attack on Gualeem, he came to Agrah, to which he immediately removed the seat of government from Dehly. And finally, when the Almighty Disposer of events thought fit in his wisdom to confer the empire of Hindûstaun upon our illustrious race, my ancestor the Emperor Bâber, after the defeat of Ibrahim, the son of Sekunder Lodi, the capture of Dehly, and subsequent reduction of Bengal, evinced his predilection for Agrah, by forming, on a spot on the opposite side of the Jumnah remarkable for the purity of the air, a spacious and magnificent garden. In one part of the garden he erected an elegant pavilion of hewn stone (green marble) of four stories, surmounted by a dome of twenty guzz in diameter,* and surrounded by a colonnade or gallery, the pillars of which were of polished marble, and the ceilings decorated with gold and lapis-lazuli, formed into beautiful figures of the most elaborate workmanship. Within the gardens, moreover, he planted a covered avenue, carried to the distance of two kôsse in length, all of sapaury trees, each of which grows to the height of fifty cubits,† the branches spreading at the top like an umbrella. In effect, for the formation of such an avenue, nothing can be better calculated than these lofty and graceful trees. In the centre of the garden (it might indeed without impropriety be called a park) he formed a basin one kôsse in circumference, the sides of which were faced all round with hewn stone, and in the centre of the basin he erected another pavilion of two stories, in which might be seated two hundred persons if necessary. The doors and walls of this also were decorated with beautiful figures of the most delicate designs, and the pavillion was approached by a convenient arched bridge of hewn stone. This garden extended altogether over a space of two hundred and fifty jerreibs,‡ and received the name of Bezugh-e-gûlaf-shaun—the rose-diffusing. In an angle of the garden he also erected a spacious mosque, with a vaulted well § attached. During the reign of the same illustrious monarch, many kinds of fruit foreign to the climate of Hindustuan were also introduced and planted in this garden. I shall mention one in particular,

* About thirty-seven feet.

† At twenty-two inches to the cubit, this would be ninety-two feet high. The saury or betel-nut is a graceful slender tree, which grows to a great height.

‡ Something less than as many acres. A jerreib is said by Richardson to be as much sown ground as will produce 768 lb. of corn, or about ten bushels.

§ Tchzajeneibah. I conjecture this to be a well of that kind which is to be seen in some parts of India, with galleries and spacious flights of steps extending from top to bottom; or perhaps it was meant to express merely a contiguous well.

cular, the ananauss* (pine-apple), being among the most delicious of those reared in the island of the Frengueis (or Portuguese); of which fruit this same garden has been known in a season to have produced nearly one hundred thousand.

Of other fruits which it produced in sufficient abundance, there were grapes of the most esteemed and delicious kinds, several kinds of apples, apricots of Suliman and Abbas, and beh-alu (some kind of plum), together with a variety of other sorts of fruits brought from Kabul and the parts of the west, hitherto strangers to the climate of Hindûstaun, but now cultivated with abundant success. Here also was introduced the sandal tree, peculiar to the islands of Zeir, or Zubberbad (*Qu.*). With regard to the Hindûstauny fruits, they were in such multiplied variety as it would be tedious to enumerate. Of flowers there was every sort of the rose, and particularly the musk and damask rose, together with the jessamin and gûltchemeily, the latter the most esteemed of Indian flowers. In short, the flowers and flowering shrubs introduced into the Gûlafshaun garden were in such endless variety as to surpass all powers of description.

The citadel or castle of Agrah, as already intimated, was rebuilt by my father from the foundation altogether of red hewn stone, with four principal entrances and two sally ports. It was, in fact, a monument of his power, so perfect in execution that one might almost venture to say it was a fabric shaped by the architect of eternal destiny from a single rock. The workmanship alone was completed at the expense of not less than one hundred and eighty-six laks of ashrefies of five methkals each.†

At the same time, emulating the example of their sovereign, every member of the court and subject of the empire, each according to his station, hastened to construct and lay out on the city and its environs mansions of the most sumptuous description, and the most beautiful gardens, so as to render the place altogether the object of universal delight and admiration. In very truth it is a wonderful city; and hence it is not surprising that in the esteem of mankind it has been placed on the same rank with Gualiar and Muttra, the latter the birth-place of *Krishna*, whom the Indian nations, in their ignorance, adore as the supreme being, and who, when they would speak in language of the highest praise, refer to these *three* places as surpassing all other cities in the known world.

I am here led to relate that at the city of Banaras a temple had been erected by Rajah Maun Sing, which cost him the sum of nearly thirty-six laks of five methkaly

* The fact is curious, as indicating that the pine was introduced into India by the Portuguese.

† Twenty-six krour and fifty-five laks of rupees, reckoning the ashrefy at fifteen rupees, that is to say, £26,550,000!

methkaly ashrefies.* The principal idol in this temple had on its head a tiara or cap, enriched with jewels to the amount of three laks of ashrefies. He had placed in this temple moreover, as the associates and ministering servants of the principal idol,† four other images of solid gold, each crowned with a tiara, in the like manner enriched with precious stones. It was the belief of these Jehennemites that a dead Hindû, provided when alive he had been a worshipper, when laid before this idol would be restored to life. As I could not possibly give credit to such a pretence, I employed a confidential person to ascertain the truth; and, as I justly supposed, the whole was detected to be an impudent imposture. Of this discovery I availed myself, and I made it my plea for throwing down the temple which was the scene of this imposture; and on the spot, with the very same materials, I erected the great mosque, because the very name of Isslâm was proscribed at Banaras, and with God's blessing it is my design, if I live, to fill it full with true believers.

On this subject I must however acknowledge, that having on one occasion asked my father the reason why he had forbidden any one to prevent or interfere with the building of these haunts of idolatry, his reply was in the following terms: "My dear child," said he, "I find myself a puissant monarch, the shadow of God upon earth. I have seen that he bestows the blessings of his gracious providence upon all his creatures without distinction. Ill should I discharge the duties of my exalted station, were I to withhold my compassion and indulgence from any of those entrusted to my charge With all of the human race, with all of God's creatures, I am at peace: why then should I permit myself, under any consideration, to be the cause of molestation or aggression to any one? Besides, are not five parts in six of mankind either Hindûs or aliens to the faith; and were I to be governed by motives of the kind suggested in your inquiry, what alternative can I have but to put them all to death! I have thought it therefore my wisest plan to let these men alone. Neither is it to be forgotten, that the class of whom we are speaking, in common with the other inhabitants of Agrah, are usefully engaged, either in the pursuits of science or the arts, or of improvements for the benefit of mankind, and have in numerous instances arrived at the highest distinctions in the state, there being, indeed, to be found in this city men of every description, and of every religion on the face of the earth."

I had been constrained to imprison my eldest son Khossrou in the upper part of the royal tower in the castle of Agrah; nevertheless, although I had received from

* Five krour and forty laks of rupees. It must be confessed that these appear to be enormous exaggerations.

† This was probably an image of Bûddâh.

from him sufficient proof of his refractory and undutiful disposition, I continued to make him a visit in his prison regularly once a month, having assigned to him, moreover, for his subsistence, the monthly sum of three laks of ashrefies, with permission that his children should visit their father once every week.

Sâeid Khaun was one of the members hereditarily attached to the service of my father, and he had been promoted by me to the government of the Punjaub, and the command of the army of Lahour. On this occasion he had received from me an elephant and dress of honour, the latter from my own wardrobe, together with a girdle and khanjar, or kreisse, enriched with jewels, also a horse and caparison and jeighah (aigrette or ornament for the turban), the two latter richly set with precious stones. This chief was of a Moghûl tribe, and his ancestors had also been long in the service of mine. Soon after he had quitted my presence, however, and had proceeded some stages on his march, it was intimated to me by some of my people, that he had among his domestics men of a cruel and tyrannical disposition, notorious for courses of oppression in various ways towards the poor and those subject to their authority. Without a moment's delay, I despatched Khaujah Saadek, the son of Mahommed Yaheya, to announce to him that as all mankind, both high and low, were equal in my contemplation, my love of justice did not permit me to overlook an act of oppression in any man. "Did the renown of Solomon surpass that of all the kings of the earth? He owed it all to the applause which he derived from his inflexible love of justice." The messenger was accordingly charged to assure them, that if from that moment there occurred the slightest proof of arbitrary proceeding among his train, the punishment would be as exemplary as it would be unmitigating. The instant this message was communicated to him, he penned an obligation in writing, which he delivered to Khaujah Saadek, purporting that if on any occasion, either in himself or any of those employed under his authority, there arose the slightest ground for a charge of oppression or injustice, his head should be the forfeit. And the engagement, thus written, he forwarded by the same Khaujah to my presence.

In order to ensure for those noble animals the regular supply of grain and water, I appointed a foujdaur, or superintendent, to every division of one thousand elephants in my train. I shall here notice, that although the elephants subsisted under my government are more in number than can be readily counted, there are twelve thousand only of a size and temper to be employed against the ranks of an enemy in the field of battle. To these must be added one thousand of a smaller size, employed to supply the larger with forage and grain. Exclusive of these must be mentioned *one hundred thousand* required to carry the amharahs, or covered litters of the females of the imperial family, and otherwise in in the conveyance of the imperial baggage, including the silver utensils, carpets, and other articles of equipage of different descriptions belonging to the imperial household. I only desire on this subject farther to remark, that this establishment of elephants was maintained at an annual expense of not less than four hundred and sixty laks of ashrefies,* exclusively of what was incurred in looking after them, each separate animal requiring fifteen persons to provide for it, and a guard of one thousand men being posted at every station of a thousand elephants.

On this subject I shall add one more circumstance, and then dismiss it altogether. One day the foujdaur of one of my elephant stations reported to me that Sûltan Ahmed, the son of Ammaudy Hûsseyne Beg, had sold an elephant of the first quality to Shûkkour Allah Beg, the son of Zeyne Khaun Koukah, for the sum of sixty thousand ashrefies:† on which information I at first determined that this Sûltan Ahmed should be thrown under the feet of an elephant and trampled to death; for by a particular regulation I had provided that no elephant of this prime description should be sold or purchased otherwise than for the use of the state. But feeling a repugnance to put any of God's people to death on such an occasion, I endeavoured to palliate the offence, and observed that this person had done well, for that every man ought to be master of his own property; my object being to lay a restraint upon all communications of this description in my presence. I accordingly admonished the foujdaur as a detractor, and assured him that if ever he introduced such a subject again in my presence, he might expect the severest punishment in my power to inflict.

Sheikh Fereid, the Bokharian, who held the appointment of Meir Bukhshy under the authority of my father, I confirmed in his appointment, bestowing upon him, according to usage, an honorary dress and scimitar set with jewels. I added at the same time, for his encouragement, an expression of the high opinion which I entertained of his merit, by pronouncing him equally competent to

D

* This cannot be otherwise than a stupendous exaggeration, for such a sum would be equivalent to the enormous aggregate of sixty-nine millions sterling! The ashrefy must therefore have been a denomination of coin of much smaller value than our estimate of fifteen rupees. Abûl Fazzel in a part of his history makes it equal to nine rupees; but it would be extravagant at almost any valuation —at a fourth part, even, it would be upwards of seventeen millions sterling! Allowing the keep of an elephant at thirty rupees a month, at the lowest, for twelve thousand elephants the expense would be three laks and sixty thousand rupees (£36,000) a month, or £432,000 per annum. On the whole, either in the enumeration of the elephants, or in the sum for their maintenance, there surely must be some extraordinary exaggeration; and this probably must lay with the person who copied the manuscript.

† This must have been the dearest of all elephants, for it must have cost nine laks of rupees, or £90,000 sterling.

to wield either the pen or the sword. I also confirmed to Mokheim Khaun the title of Vezzeir Khaun, bestowed upon him by my father, with the functions of Vezzeir annexed to the title. I appointed Khaujeki Futtah-ullah to be steward of my household. To Abdurrezauk Maaonmoury (the architect), who had formerly deserted my service and sought my father's protection, by whom he had been placed in the rank of Bukhshy, I assigned the same rank in my armies; giving him at the same time a khellaut (pellise) or dress of honour. In short, whether within the household or without, I not only permitted those who held places of trust or dignity about my father's court to retain their appointments, but to all, according to their respective degrees, gave advancement in rank and station.

Upon Sherreif Khaun, the son of Abdulhamid Messower (the portrait painter) who had grown up with me from infancy to manhood, and to whom, while yet but heir apparent, I had already given the title of Khaun, I conferred the dignity of Ameir-ul-Oomra, or premier grandee of the empire. And this entirely in consideration of his devoted attachment to my person, which is of that exalted degree, that I know not whether to esteem him most as a brother, friend, or son, or companion and inseparable associate: nay, I do not know but that I consider him as dear to me as one of the members of my own body. Upon the whole, as far as I am capable of judging, there is not to be found, in all the armies of this mighty empire, his equal, either in talent or experience; and yet I most solemnly aver, that although it has often been with me the subject of deep reflection, I have never been able to devise any title, station, or dignity that could be at all adequate to the opinion which I entertain of his exalted merit. It is however to be observed, that while my father reigned, it was the rule never to promote the greatest Ameirs beyond the command of five thousand, because it is to be apprehended the man who sees at his back a numerous body of warriors, and any deficiency in that respect on the part of his sovereign, seldom fails to play the traitor, and to involve himself in the mazes of rebellion. This rule of my father's government I considered it expedient to maintain, and I accordingly limited his promotion to the command of five thousand only. Nevertheless, I am still persuaded that the commanding of five thousand is far short of what is due to the dignity of Ameir-ul-Oomra, a premier grandee of the empire. I have apprized him that all that belongs to me is at his disposal; and as to rank, he has limited his ambition to whatever in the spirit of kindness I may think proper to bestow upon him. More than this, he has frequently assured me, that while he is before the world, that is, engaged in public life, he would never accept from me of any rank beyond that of five thousand: to which I have yielded my reluctant assent.

While

While I am on this subject I must further relate, that at the crisis of my return from Allahabad to the province of my father, of which hereafter, among the several Ameirs who accompanied me of whose fidelity I felt most assured, Sherreif Khaun was the man. And sixteen days after my accession, when he came to offer me his pledge of services, I can with a safe conscience aver, that the same day on which he thus made his appearance in my presence, God Almighty bestowed upon me a renewal of life, and I felt at the moment convinced that the eye of his providence was upon me. I felt indeed an assurance that, possessing the attachment of the Ameir-ul-Oomra alone, I was in very truth the sovereign of my people: for although at the time not exactly aware of any circumstances of doubt or danger, there was this conviction, that at the risk of life itself, Sherreif Khaun would be my defender. God is, indeed, equally the protector of all his creatures: yet is the possession of self-knowledge, of all things, to sovereigns the most indispensable. Such, at all events, I know to be the zeal and purity of the Ameir-ul-Oomra's attachment towards me, that when at last I dismissed him to the government of Bengal, over which I invested him with paramount authority, and confirmed to him his rank of five thousand, together with the great drum and standard, the day on which he was finally removed from my presence was one of the blackest of my life. I shall dwell no further on this subject than to add, that the father of Sherreif Khaun was a native of Shirâz, and his grandfather was Nizam-ul-Moulk, the Vezzeir of Shah Shuja, the sovereign of that state. His father was admitted to the intimate society of my grandfather Homayûn, and held, moreover, some of the highest dignities about the court of my father, being by the mother's side a sherreif, or descendant from the Prophet. An account of all these circumstances will, however, be found at large in the Zuffernâmah and Mûtlaa-ul-Saadein.

Certain considerations, nevertheless, prevailed with me some time afterwards to reinstate the Rajah Maun Sing in the government of Bengal, although he could himself have entertained no expectations of such a favour at my hands. I conferred upon him at the same time an honorary dress, or pellise, and a scimitar set with jewels, together with the horse Koukpárah, the best in my thousand-ashref horse stables. The first of the Râjpoot chieftains who became attached to the government of my father Akbar was Bharmul, the grandfather of this Rajah Maun Sing, and pre-eminent in his tribe for courage, fidelity, and truth. As a mark of distinguished favour, my father placed the daughter of Rajah Bharmul in his own palace, and finally espoused her to me. It was by this princess I had my son Khossrou. I was then only seventeen, and he is now twenty; and I trust that God Almighty may yet prolong his life to the age of one hundred and twenty: for as I have *hitherto* had every reason to be satisfied

 with

with his conduct, so also do I hope that it will always be such as to deserve the approbation of his God: certainly, to *this day*, I have not experienced aught at his hands but the strictest fidelity and attachment.* My first child was, however, a sister of Khossrou's by the same mother, and a year older than Khossrou.

After Khossrou, by the daughter of Sâeid Khaun, the son of Sultûn Saurung prince of Kashobar, I had a daughter, to whom we gave the name of Ouffet Baunee Begum. She died at the age of three years. Next to her, by Sauheb Jamaul, the neice of Zeyne Khaun Khoukah, I had a son born at Kabûl, on whom my father bestowed the name of Parveiz. Of him I pray God that he may live to the utmost limit of human life, since from the singular activity and ready zeal of his character I cherish of him the very highest expectations. The first servive on which I thought fit to employ him is one of a religious nature against the Râna (of Oudipour); and it is now the four-and-twentieth month since he was despatched. It is very gratifying to find that the Ameirs appointed to serve under his orders all express themselves entirely satisfied with his conduct. He has with him nearly twenty thousand cavalry, all furnished with three spare horses each.

Next by the daughter of Derya Komm, a powerful Rajah at the foot of the mountains of Lahour, I had a daughter born, to whom I gave the name of Doulut Nisha Begum, who died at the age of seven months. Then another daughter by Beiby Karmitty, of the family of Râey Pour, whom I named Bahar Baunu Begum: she lived only two months. Next by Juggut Gossâeine, the daughter of Rajah Oudi Sing, who was master of eighty thousand horse, and than whom among the Rajahs of Hind there were few more powerful, I had another daughter, who received the name of Begum Sûltaun, but who did not survive her twelve months. By Sauheb Jamaul, who was the daughter of the Rajah of Luknou, came also a daughter, who lived only seven days; and by the daughter of Moûtah Rajah† (Juggut Gossâeine) was born my son Khorroum.‡ Possessed as he is of the brightest intellectual endowments, I cannot but hope, with the blessing of God, that in every virtue and good quality this my son may prove uninterruptedly progressive, as he is in all things conspicuously discreet. In attention to my father he exceeded all my children, and he was accordingly by him beloved beyond all others, my father repeatedly expressing to me, that such qualities as he discovered in him were not to be found in any other of my children. Perhaps being then the youngest of all, he might have appeared in the eyes of every one the loveliest.

After him, by the daughter of the prince of Kashmeir, who was of the society of

* Not more than six months after this we shall find him, nevertheless, in arms against his panegyrist; and certainly there are some previous proofs not very advantageous to his filial character.

† The *fat* Rajah, title of Oudi Sing. ‡ Afterwards the Emperor Shahjahaun.

of Jouggies, I had another daughter, who died a year old. Then by Shâei Begum, the daughter of Ibrauhim Hûsseyne Mirza, who was the grandson by a daughter of Mirza Kamraun, I had another daughter, who died before she was eight months old. Again, by Sauheb Jamaul, the mother of Parveiz, I had another daughter, who died at the age of five months. After her, by Juggut Gossâeine, the mother of Khorroum, I had a daughter, to whom I gave the name of Luzzet-ul-Nissa Begum : she died, however, at the age of five years. Again, by the mother of Parveiz I had another son, to whom, at my accession to the throne, they gave the name of Jahaundar; and last of all, by the mother of Khorroum I had another son, who received the name of Sheheryaur : both of these were born in the same month.

Having by his matrimonial alliances, already indicated,* considerably augmented his influence, Maun Sing obtained such a predominance in my father's government, that he was permitted to reside alternately six months at court and six months at his jagueir. As a proof of the affluence of his resources it is sufficient to state, that whenever he repaired to my father's presence, it seldom occurred that his compliment of homage did not amount to two laks of five mithkaly ashrefies ;† and so far did he outstrip all tha this grandfather, Bharmul, had attained to, that among the Rajahs of Hindustaun there is not one that can be put on a parrallel with Rajah Maun Sing.

Another circumstance which I consider not unworthy of relation is the following. Sâeid Khaun, the governor of the Punjaub, had written to me a shortish note, requesting that Ghauze Beg, the son of Mirza Jaun Beg, might be permitted to repair to him without delay, as he had just adopted him as a son. I informed him in reply, that my father Akbar had entered into preliminaries of a matrimonial alliance with the Ghauze Beg, by which his sister was betrothed to my son Khossrou, and as that contract was fulfilled he would be permitted to depart. I should explain that the Mirza Jaun, or Jauny Beg, here referred to, was the son of Fayendah Mahommed, the son of Mirza Bâky, the son of Mirza Aaby, son of Abdul Aaly Terkhan. This latter was prince of Bokhâra in the time of Sûltan Mirza, and long numbered among his vassals the celebrated Shâhy Beg Khaun, monarch of the Ouzbeks, and many of his kinsmen. Abdul Aaly Terkhan was, moreover, descended from Shukkee Beg Terkhan, who had this title conferred upon him while yet a child, by the invincible Teymûr,

* The daughter of Rajah Bharmul was probably his sister ; she was, as we have seen, the mother of Jahangueir's eldest son Khossrou.

† The value of the ashrefy is so problematical, that I am not yet able to speak with precision. A passage in the second volume of Abûl Fazzel's history makes it equal to nine rupees ; the present here spoken of would therefore be equivalent to eighteen laks of rupees, or £180,000 sterling.

Teymûr, his father Eygou Teymûr having fallen in battle in the war with Toktemesh Khaun. They were of the race of Arghûn Khaun, and hence the title of Terkhan and Arghûn.

An application was conveyed to me in behalf of the son of Rajah Muksoud Khaun, the son of Mukhsous Khaun, so long engaged in the rebel transactions in Bengal and Bahâr. I caused it to be answered in reply, that as he could not well be in a state of mind to be quite satisfied with me, neither could I consider him a fit object for the goodness of God, nor for the countenance or encouragement of an earthly sovereign.

Having instructed a commission of religious persons to arrange for me a collection of the simple names of God, as far as they could discover, they furnished me with a list of five hundred and twenty-two, exactly double the number of those contained in my royal father's sacred rosary. They arranged these five hundred and twenty-two names under twenty numerical letters (abjed), which I caused to be inscribed (perhaps embroidered) in my mantle.* The evening of Friday throughout the year I devoted invariably to the society of the learned, and of pious and virtuous men of every description. For a twelvemonth prior to my accession to sovereign power I had adopted a resolution, on that evening never, on any consideration, to taste either of wine or any intoxicating beverage whatever. I trust in Providence to enable me to abide by this resolution to the last moment of my existence, even to the awful day of universal reckoning. Hitherto the Almighty has given me grace to persevere in it, and may the same grace be continued to me for the remainder of my life.

I encouraged such individuals as were immediately in attendance about my person, whenever it was found that the stipend was inadequate to their station, and the circumstance should have escaped my own observation, to make known the deficiency to me, in order that the allowance might be respectively increased according to necessity. I gave orders that, until the period of mourning for my father should have expired, the people should abstain from every species of sustenance but that dew made use of by the Souffies. During the same period I also directed that in the celebration of marriage ceremonies, neither drum, nor trumpet, nor any other description of music should be employed in any part of the dominions subject to my authority, on pain of heavy displeasure.

While this ordinance was yet in force, a report was brought to me that a certain Hâkim Ally was celebrating the marriage of his son, and that in the entertainment which he was giving on the occasion, he had assembled at his house in the presence of the Kauzy the whole of a band of music belonging to Killidje Khaun, and that in fact the whole city resounded with the noise. I despatched Mahommed

* In the manuscript this is entirely unintelligible; it is however probably reddâi, a mantle or cloak.

Mahommed Tekky to remind him, that as his obligations to the bounty of my father were great, it might have been expected that he, beyond all other men, would have been overwhelmed with grief, shame, and sorrow: was this then the only period which he could find for the marriage of his son, and its noisy festivities? When the messenger appeared among them the party seemed absorbed in all the intoxication of mirth and jollity; but when the message was delivered, it was amusing to see the sudden change into confusion and dismay. Penetrated with remorse for such a proof of thoughtless levity, the same Hâkim Ally, as an atonement, brought me a chaplet of pearl of the value of a lak of rupees, of which at the moment I condescended to accept; but some days afterwards, sending for him to my presence, I threw the chaplet round his neck. It never could, in truth, afford me any real gratification to receive from any vassals gifts or presents in any shape: on the contrary, towards my hand should their eyes ever be turned; and so long as I retain the means, so long is it my part to bestow upon every one favour and rewards according to merit.

I bestowed upon Mahommed Khaun, now appointed to succeed to the government of the Punjaub, the donation of one lak of rupees, together with a costly dress, and a scimitar, belt, and dagger, all richly set with diamonds and other precious stones. This chief is of the family of the khauns of Ferrah. About the same time I despatched Mahommed Rezza with fifty thousand rupees, to be distributed among the poor and other inmates of the sacred or consecrated places at Dehly. I conferred the office of vezzeir of the empire upon Vezzeir Khaun, having, while yet only first prince of the blood, already bestowed upon him the title of Vezzeir-ul-Moulk, and advanced him from the command of five hundred to that of one thousand horse.

It is to be remembered that Sheikh Fereid Bokhaury was of the stock of Sheikh Jullaul, who was a distinguished disciple of Sheikh Behâ-ud-dein Zekkareïah of Multân. The ancestor in the fourth degree of Sheikh Fereid was Seyed Abdul Ghoffaur of Dehly; and this latter had bequeathed it to his children as an irrevocable charge, never to engage themselves as civil stipendiaries, but to devote their services entirely to the hazards of a military life. They are illustrious among the Seyeds of Bokhara. Sheikh Fereid had previously held the rank of four thousand, but I advanced him to that of five thousand, with the appendages of the great drum and standard.

To Mirza Rûstum, the son of Mirza Sûltan Hûsseyne, governor of Kandahâr; to Abdurrahim Khaun, who bears the title of Khaun Khanan, and who is the son of Beiram Khaun Kuzzelbaush (red cap);* and to his two sons, Eiridje and Darab;

* This is rather a contemptuous appellation for the illustrious first minister of Akbar; it is the designation of any ordinary Persian.

Darab; and lastly, to Sheir Khojah, of the family of Mirza Ally Beg Akbar-shâhy, I transmitted respectively, suitable to their rank, the proper khelauts, or dresses of honour, together with baldrics and swords enriched with precious stones, and horses with caparisons enriched in the same manner.* The son of Abdurrahman Vaeg, on the contrary, who had left his post without invitation, I ordered back in displeasure: for the best proof of zeal is obedience, not verbal profession.

Lâla Beg, the Kabûlite, had received from me, previous to my accession, the title of Bauz Bahauder; but about a month subsequent to my ascending the throne, coming to render homage to me, I raised him from the rank of one thousand to that of two thousand horse, and invested him in the government of Bahâr, presenting him at the same time with a donation of one lak of rupees; the feudatories of the provinces, of whatever rank, being publicly apprized that it was at the discretion of Bauz Bahauder to put any to death who disobeyed or resisted his authority. I provided moreover that his jaguir, or fee, should be of a higher value than that of any of his subordinates; for I could not but bear in mind that he belonged to that class of the soldiery most faithfully devoted to my family. His father, I must observe, bore the name of Nizam-e-kabaub,† and he was Chirâghtchei, or conductor of the flambeaux, or lamplighter to my uncle.

To the only son of the deceased Mahommed Hakaim Mirza of Kabûl, who previously held the rank of five hundred, I now gave that of one thousand; and Kanûjen, a Raujpout Mahratta, distinguished beyond his equals for loyalty towards my person, I raised from the rank of eight hundred to that of fifteen hundred horses.

Meiran Suddur-ud-dein, who held the rank of three hundred only, I advanced to that of a thousand. This person was one of the oldest on the list of my father's servants, and at the period when Sheikh Abdul Nebby was instructing me to read the *forty traditions*, was employed in the imperial library. In truth I can allege, that I ever looked upon him as my khalifah, or supreme pontiff. But in my father's esteem no person held so lofty a place as my preceptor Abdul Nebby; unless it were, indeed, Mekhdoum-ul-Moulk, whose original name was Sheikh Abdullah, and who in science, good sense, and narrative eloquence, was without his equal in the age in which he lived. He was a man far advanced in years, and had in early life possessed unbounded influence with Sheir Khaun the Afghan, and his son Seleim Khaun. He was, moreover, unrivalled in his knowledge

* Most probably these articles were coronation presents.

† Director of the kitchen. *Kabaub*, a well known article in Oriental cookery.

ledge of the heavenly bodies : and yet his star did not brighten in the esteem of my father. In the end, Sheikh Abdul Nebby gained the advance.

When Hakim Hammaum was appointed on his embassy to Ma-wer-un-neher, (Transoxiana), Meiran Suddur Jahaun (the same referred to as Suddur-ud-dein) was despatched on the mission of condolence on the death of the father of Abdullah Khaun, monarch of the Ouzbeks. On his return after an absence of three years, my father thought fit to place him in a military station ; and he was at different periods advanced to the rank or two thousand, and to the important trust of suddur, or grand almoner of the empire. I shall finally observe that, under whatever change of circumstance, Meiran Suddur Jahaun has always evinced an unabated zeal in his attachment to my interests ; neither is he in any degree deficient in any of the qualities of true courage and virtue : and it might be truly said that his affection towards me was a sentiment implanted in his heart from his very cradle, so meritoriously has he ever discharged the claims of gratitude and true loyalty. When yet only prince royal, I had freely engaged either to advance him to any rank he might require, or to discharge for him any debts he might have contracted, to whatever amount. In fulfilment of such engagement, when placed by Omnipotence on the throne of Hindûstaun, I communicated to him accordingly, that I was prepared to make good my promise in either of the alternatives that he might determine upon. The bukhshies of my court announced to me in reply from the Suddur, that if the command of four thousand were conferred upon him, he would trust to his own resources for the liquidation of his debts.

In compliance with this request, although at variance with the rule which I had prescribed myself, never in the first instance to bestow a higher rank than that of one hundred, I created him a grandee of the class of four thousand. In truth, considering the heart as the genuine seat of true devotion, I esteem the securing to myself of one such faithful heart not inferior in merit to a thousand grand pilgrimages to the sacred cities. Neither would I neglect, so far as compliance rests within my power, to fulfil the just expectations of any man, without distinction of infidel or true believer. This age-stricken ruin of a world has survived hundreds of thousands such as I am ; what then can be more desirable than to do something in the fleeting present, of the merit of which we may avail ourselves in an eternal hereafter ? Even in this world, the advantages of a benevolent action, of gaining to ourselves the attachment of mankind, are beyond all price ; and for my part, I should derive a greater satisfaction from rejoicing the heart of a single individual, than from leaving behind me jewels and gold by the horse-load, to be squandered by a profligate heir.

 Remember,

Remember, my son, that this world is no permanent possession. It offers no resting-place, either for reliance or hope. Hast thou not heard how in the chambers of the west, the throne of Solomon was delivered to the winds; of that Solomon the blessed of all generations. Thrice happy the man whose life has been passed in the practice of wisdom and justice, whose exertions have been directed to the repose of mankind; he bears away the honours of the course. The wise man's care is devoted to the duties of his religion; but, whatever your pursuits, the world is slipping away. That alone is useful which you can carry to the grave, not that which you have hoarded, and must be left behind you. Let your business be to secure the approbation of the experienced, for though the huntsman has his skill, the old wolf has his cunning. Hast thou a contest with thine adversary, oppose him with thy bravest hearts; the tiger alone is competent to a conflict with the lion. Be not afraid of the young soldier, however sharp his sword; beware of the veteran, with his skill in battle often tried. The young man may have strength to wrestle with the lion and the elephant, but where is his experience in the guile of the year-worn fox? Man acquires prudence by seeing the world at large, byfeeling alternately the effects of heat and cold. Wouldst thou see thy country flourishing and happy, trust not an affair of importance to the discretion of an upstart. In a matter where there is peril employ none others than soldiers tried in many a battle. The true-bred hound quails not before the tiger; the fox will venture battle where the lion is unseen. Train up thy son in the exertion of the chase, and when the day of battle arrives he will subdue his fears. Even the bravest man, when wearied in the lap of indulgence, trembles when the approaches of battle are thrown open to him. Two men there are with whom we should not disgrace the back of the war-horse, and whom the hand of an infant would strike to the earth: one of whom in battle you have seen the back, and whom you should slay with the sword, if perchance he may have escaped that of the enemy. Better is the coward confessed, than the man of the sword who in the course of the conflict turns away his head like a woman.

Of Mirza Gheyauss Beg* how shall I speak in terms of sufficient praise! With the office of high steward of the household he had enjoyed, under my father, the dignity of a grandee of one thousand; and I appointed him, some time after my accession, to the office of diwan or chancellor, in the room of Vezzeir Khaun, with the rank of *seven* thousand, the title of Ettemaud-ud-Doulah, and the insignia of the great drum and standard. In the science of arithmetic he is in this age without a rival; in composition and elegance of style he stands alone; in critical knowledge on every species of the poetry of former

* Ghaja Aiass, according to Dow.

former ages, and the facility with which he quotes from it, he has no competitor; and few are diwans, or collections of odes, which he has not preserved, and of which he has not transcribed the most beautiful and esteemed. But what is better in the proof than a thousand mûferra yakouties,* the recitation is never made without a countenance beaming with smiles. I can only add, that in affairs of state, the measure which has not the confirmation of his counsels, has little chance, from the imperfection of its arrangements, to remain upon the record.

[Here follow five couplets in praise of the virtues of Ettemaud-ud-Doulah, which it would be tedious to insert.]

Ettemaud-ud-Doulah, it is almost superfluous to observe, is the father of my consort Nourjahaun Begum and of Assof Khan, whom I have appointed my lieutenant-general, with the rank of a commander of *five thousand.* On Nourjahaun, however, who is the superior of the four hundred inmates of my harram, I have conferred the rank of *thirty thousand.* In the whole empire there is scarcely a city in which this princess has not left some lofty structure, some spacious garden, as a splendid monument of her taste and munificence. As I had then no intention of marriage, she did not originally come into my family, but was betrothed in the time of my father to Sheer Afkunn; but when that *chief was killed,*† I sent for the Kauzy, and contracted a regular marriage with her, assigning for her dowry the sum of eighty laks of ashrefies of five methkals,‡ which sum she requested as indispensable for the purchase of jewels, and I granted it without a murmur. I presented her, moreover, with a necklace of pearl, containing forty beads, each of which had cost me separately the sum of forty thousand rupees.§ At the period in which this is written, I may say that the whole concern of my household, whether gold or jewels, is under her sole and entire management.|| Of my unreserved confidence, indeed, this princess is in entire possession, and I may allege without a fallacy, that the whole fortune of my empire has been consigned to the disposal of this highly endowed family; the father being my diwan, the son my lieutenant-general, with unlimited powers, and the daughter the inseparable companion of all my cares.

In

* In Richardson's Dictionary reference is made to a cordial or exhilarating prescription thus designated, the ingredients of which consist partly of rubies.

† Notoriously by the contrivance of the worthy monarch himself. The story is something like that of King David and Bathsheba.

‡ Seven krour and twenty laks of rupees, or £7,200,000; one of those enormous sums which startles belief!

§ Sixteen laks of rupees, or about £160,000.

|| A passage occurs in this place of eight or nine words only which it is difficult to decypher; but it seems to refer to some revenue or advantage derived from the cultivation or sale of opium.

In the next place, I invested the son of Rajah Bikramajit, who bore the title of Râi Râyan, with the important appointment of master of ordnance, or superintendant of my department of artillery; and I directed that, independently of such as were distributed in various parts of my dominions, either in guns or gunners, there should, in this department, always be ready for service sixty thousand camel-mounted guns, each supplied with ten seirs of powder and twenty shot; and twenty thousand other pieces (perhaps of larger calibre) with every requisite equipment. To defray the expense of such an establishment altogether, I set apart fifteen purgunnahs or townships, yielding a revenue of one lak,* or five daunky ashrefies. This equipment was to accompany the imperial camp whithersoever it moved.

The Râi Râyan had for some time held the appointment of Diwan under my father Akbar, and is one of his oldest dependents; he is now far advanced in years, and in proportion possessed of the most extensive experience, not less in the regulations of civil policy than in the management of martial discipline, on which he may be said to be master of the *six* parts complete. Together with his experience, he accumulated under my father treasure to an immense amount, in gold; so great, indeed, that even among the Hindûs of his class he has not his equal in wealth, since he is known, at the period in which I am writing, to have at a time, in the hands of certain merchants of his caste in the city, no less than ten krours of ashrefies.† From the superintendence of the elephant department, he is now advanced to the dignity of Vezzeir-ul-Oomra.

I availed myself of an opportunity to promote Seyed Kammaul, the son of Seyed Chaund the Bokhârian, from the command of seven hundred to that of one thousand, and assigning for his jaguir the city of Dehly, the metropolis of the ancient monarchs of Hindûstaun. The father of Seyed Kammaul had been killed at Peishawer, in the war with the Afghans. I further advanced Mirza Khorrem, the son of Kherun-e-Azzem, from the rank of two thousand to that of three thousand horse.

In the practice of being burnt on the funeral pyre of their husbands, as sometimes exhibited among the widows of the Hindûs, I had previously directed, that no woman who was the mother of children should be thus made a sacrifice, however willing to die; and I now further ordained, that in no case was the practice to be permitted, when compulsion was in the slightest degree employed, whatever might be the opinions of the people. In other respects they were in no

* Nine lacs of rupees, or £90,200, which would be utterly inadequate to the expense of such an establishment.

† Ninety krour of rupees, or £90,000,000! an enormous sum, and beyond all credibility.

no wise to be molested in the duties of their religion, nor exposed to oppression or violence in any manner whatever. For when I consider that the Almighty has constituted me the shadow of his beneficence on earth, and that his gracious providence is equally extended to all existence, it would but ill accord with the character thus bestowed, to contemplate for an instant the butchery of nearly a whole people; for of the whole population of Hindûstaun, it is notorious that five parts in six are composed of Hindûs,* the adorers of images, and the whole concerns of trade and manufactures, weaving, and other industrious and lucrative pursuits, are entirely under the management of these classes. Were it, therefore, ever so much my desire to convert them to the true faith, it would be impossible, otherwise than through the excision of millions of men. Attached as they thus are to their religion, such as it is, they will be snared in the web of their own inventions: they cannot escape the retribution prepared for them; but the massacre of a whole people can never be any business of mine.

Among other regulations of minor importance, I directed, that when any individual of a respectable class in the service of the state was desirous of visiting the country of his birth, application should be made through Sheikh Fereid, the Meir Bukhshy, when permission would be given without difficulty.

It had been usual to send the patents of jaguir in vermillion. I directed that for the future this should be done in gold.

I conferred upon Vezzeir Khaun the appointment of Diwan, or comptroller of finance in Bengal, with unlimited authority; and I despatched him into that province, for the purpose of investigating the state of the revenue, of which for ten years past no correct account had been received.

Mirza Sûltân, the son of Mirza Shahrokh, prince of Badakhshaun, being the most accomplished of the children of his father, I ever considered as a son of my own, and as such placed him under the care of the Ameer-ul-Oomrah, as the highest in rank in the empire. I referred the claims of Mirza Shemsy, the son of Khaun-e-Azzem, with instructions to investigate the truth, to Bauz Bahauder. To gratify the wishes of his father, I bestowed the rank of a grandee of fifteen hundred on Bhaou Sing, the son of Rajah Maun Sing. He was the only surviving son, although the latter is known to have had by his fifteen hundred wives not less than two and three children each, all of whom died except this one: neither was he possessed of sufficient ability to qualify him to be his father's successor. Nevertheless, in this instance, I was induced to promote him. He was a commander of five hundred in the court of my father.

Zemaunah

* It is curious to remark, that the same proportion appears to exist at this day, since Bishop Heber, in his interesting Journal, observes, that the Mahommedans in India bear to the Hindûs the same proportion as the Protestants to the Roman Catholics in Ireland.

Zemaunah Beg, the son of Ghour Beg the Kabûlite, had been in my service from childhood, and previous to my accession had received from me the rank of five hundred; I now bestowed upon him the title of Mohaubet Khaun, with the rank of fifteen hundred, and the appointment of Vezzeir of the Shagird Beishah, provost of the apprentices, perhaps director of the manufactures. I also gave to Zeya-ud-dein the Kazvinian the rank of one thousand.

For distribution among my cavalry and other retainers I directed Bikkendas, the keeper of the stables, to bring into my presence two hundred horses every day; for it were a thousand pities to have in my retinue any number of horses, either lame or worn down by age or hard labour.

On the 11th day of the month of Shabaun, of the year one thousand and nineteen, * I bestowed the daughter of Mirza Rûstam, the grandson of Behram Mirza, upon my favourite son Parveiz, with a marriage portion of one lak of ashrefies. † At the entertainment given on the occasion, the richest and most splendid dresses were distributed to the Ameirs and others permitted to be present, and nearly one hundred maunns Hindy of frankincense, sandal, musk, ambergris, and other aromatic drugs, were consumed during the ceremony. The consumption in other articles may be estimated from this statement. On the evening on which the bride was brought to the palace, I presented her with a necklace of sixty pearls, for each single pearl of which my father had paid the sum of ten thousand rupees. ‡ I also presented them with a ruby of the value of two laks and fifty thousand rupees, equivalent to seven thousand tomauns of Irâk;§ and I finally assigned for her expenses the annual sum of three laks of rupees, and for the establishment of her household one hundred maidens from Surat, who were devoted to her service.

I promoted Mirza Ally Akbar Shâhy to the rank of four thousand, and sent him to command on the frontiers of Kashmeir, giving him at the same time an enaum or premium of one lak of rupees, together with a valuable charger and saddle set with jewels, enriched girdle and dagger, and a jeighah, or aigrette, for the turban.

Bauker Khaun Nûdjûm Sâni, who held under my father the humble rank of a command of three hundred only, I advanced by degrees to the dignity of two thousand, and finally invested him with the government of Mûltan, assigning to him the foujdaury, or military command on the river Ally Khan, and over the districts in that quarter. More than this, I destined the sister's child as Nourja-haun

* 18th of September, A.D. 1610.

† Nine laks of rupees, or £90,000.

‡ Six laks of rupees, equal to £60,000 sterling.

§ About £25,000.

haun Begum for his bride, giving him the appellation of son, which I caused to be inserted in the patent for his appointment. In his profession of a soldier he is most distinguished for courage and intrepidity, and I have it in mind to avail myself of every opportunity to advance him in rank and dignity.

With a gratuity of three thousand rupees I committed to Rana Sing the superintendance of my father's tomb, which is three kôsse to the westward of the city of Agrah;* my Ameirs, of whatever degree, being enjoined on coming to court, first of all to offer homage on that consecrated spot, after which only they would be permitted to do the same in my presence.

Upon receiving a hint one day from the Ameir-ul-Oomra, which concurred most exactly with the suggestions of my own mind, I established as a rule, that no one was to be entrusted with the transaction of any concern of my government until his qualifications were first tried by the touchstone of experience, in order to form something like an estimate how far in his hands it was likely to be brought to a favourable issue. A matter of importance can, indeed, never be expected to succeed in the hands of a blockhead; and to engage a man of ability in the transaction of a trifle, would be to let fly a hawk against a mosquito. Without some considerations of this nature the business of any state must soon fall into confusion; and the welfare and regularity of every government must always greatly depend upon the character of those who are retained about the person of the sovereign. [Here follow four couplets so perversely transcribed as be scarcely legible].

At the period at which I am writing, information reached me that Samarkand, lately under the authority of Bauky Khaun the Ouzbek, had devolved to a chief of the name of Wally Khâun, and as it was the outset of his power, I conceived it possible that he might have placed himself in a position of hostility towards me. In that case I had at first determined to send my son Parveiz to oppose him, with the design at a future period for once at least to proceed, God willing, in person into Ma-wer-un-neher (Transoxiana), that is after I should have accomplished my plans for invading the Dekkan, or south of India. For I had had it long in contemplation to advance the standard of victory into the provinces in that quarter, and having there brought my designs to a successful issue, then to conduct my triumphant legions towards Samarkand. This inclination I derived from my father, who had always cherished a longing for the inheritance of his ancestors; but aware of the impolicy of leaving India unfurnished with troops to the discretion of any son, I resolved to employ Parveiz once more against the Râna of Oudipour, assigning that country in jaguir to him; those of Mûltan and

* At Sekundera. See a description of this splended edifice in A.D. 1825, in the journal of the lamented and excellent Bishop Heber.

and Agrah being transferred to others. Thus, should it please God to give me complete relief from my anxieties on this head, I might be at liberty this same year to bend my course into the Dekkan; or should the Râna, misled by his evil destiny, still continue refractory, the same force assembled under my immediate authority, might be promptly employed to destroy him root and branch.

Among the Ameirs whom I detached under the orders of Parveiz the most distinguished was Assof Khaun, who had been the vezzeir of my father, and whom I now raised to the order of five thousand, with the insignia of the standard and great drum, or naggarah. He received at the same time a scimitar enriched with diamonds, a war elephant, and a charger with enriched caparisons. I devolved to him on this occasion the appointment of atabek, or governor, to my son. Assof Khaun bore originally the name of Jauffer Beg, and was a native of Kazvein, the son of Baddeia-uz-zemman, who was the son of Aga Bellaul, who was enrolled among the vezzeirs of the departed Shah Tahmasp (of Persia). The title of Assof Khaun was conferred upon him by my father, to whom he was first of all Meir Bukhshy; but from his extraordinary talents and experience, he became soon advanced to the dignity of vezzeir, an office which for two years he held with unlimited powers. Pre-eminent in intellectual endowments and acuteness of sagacity, I raised him from the class of vezzeirs to that of ameir. On the occasion I issued strict injunctions to all the functionaries, of whatever class or degree, to abide without demur or deviation by his decisions, which I was assured would ever be governed by the purest principles of zeal and integrity.

At the same time I sent to Shahzadah Parveiz a chaplet of pearl of the value of five laks of rupees, with instructions to build in the Râna's territory a city equal to Banaras, to which he was to give the name of *Parvizabád*. I appointed Abdurrezzak Maammoury (the architect), with the rank of one thousand, to the office of Bukhshy to the Shahzadah, permitting Mokhtaur Beg, the uncle of Assof Khaun, who held the rank of commander of eight hundred horse, to accompany the prince my son. To Sheikh Rokn-ud-dein the Afghan, I had given the title of Sheir Khaun, previous to my accession to the throne; and I here only desire to remark that he was a man of undoubted courage, but happening to engage in the service of some of the Kashmirian chiefs, he became strongly addicted to habits of drinking, although, nevertheless, a man of singular and the soundest discretion.

I shall here record the elevation by me to the dignity of a commander of two thousand horse, of Sheikh Abdurrahman, the son of Abûl Fazzel, although the father was well known to me as a man of profligate principles. For towards the close of my father's reign, availing himself of the influence which by some means or or other he had acquired, he so wrought upon the mind of his master, as to instil into him the belief that the seal and asylum of prophecy, to whom the devotion of a thousand lives such as mine would be a sacrifice too inadequate to speak of, was no more to be thought of than as an Arab of singular eloquence, and that the sacred inspirations recorded in the Korân were nothing else but fabrications invented by the ever-blessed Mahommed. Actuated by these reasons it was *that I employed the man who killed* Abûl Fazzel and brought his head to me, and for this it was that I incurred my father's deep displeasure.* Hence also it was that I solemnly appealed to the Prophet's sacred name, and ventured to proclaim that, with his assistance, I should still make my way good to the throne of Hindûstaun. I am compelled to add, that under the influence of his displeasure on this occasion, my father gave to my son Khossrou, over me, every advantage of rank and favour, explicitly declaring that after him *Khossrou should be king*. Sheikh Saadi has long since pronounced, "God will dispose of him whom he has destined to take away, though the atheist may himself pretend to shroud the body." In the end, the Almighty brought his purposes to a consummation. After the death of Abûl Fazzel, however, my father became impressed with other notions, and returning again a little into the right way, shewed himself once more an orthodox believer.

To the dignity of a commander of two thousand I also raised Zauhed Khaun, the son of Saadek Mahommed Khaun, the vezzeir of Kara Khaun the Tûrkmaun. Under the authority of my father this person had discharged the duties of general of artillery, and at the seige of Asseire, had eminently distinguished himself by his activity and skill, which were indeed the grounds for his present advancement. I presented him at the same time with bûzûrg audem,† and a donation of thirty thousand rupees.

I should mention, in passing, that Râi Mûnnouher, of the Hindû tribe of Ketchwa, was a person on whom, in early youth, my father had bestowed numerous marks of kindness, and with whom he was accustomed to converse in Persian. He is indeed a man possessed of extensive general knowledge, and still established in the service of the monarchy. He has on some occasions given proofs of a turn for the poetry of Arabia of no mean merit. One stanza of his contains the following sentiment: "Wouldst thou learn the object of the rich pelisse? it is this—no one shall put out his feet in the presence of the lion." In this tribe, however, we must not look for brilliancy of imagination.

F Pahar

* It was always suspected that Jahangueir was deeply implicated in the murder of the elegant historian of his father's reign; but here is the cold-blooded acknowledgment at full length!

† According to some authorities *audem* signifies a ruby, in which case the article presented would be a large ruby.

Pahar Khaun was a dignitary of two thousand, and the uncle of Râjah Maun Sing. He was a man inclined to habits of retirement, although by no means deficient in military talent and the art of war. One of his sisters was in my father's harram, but no favourite with destiny, although possessed of uncommon beauty. The proverb says: "If there be any auspicious destiny it is for the ill-favoured, for from all I can observe in this workshop of creation, scarcely any thing appears in its proper place. The poor in spirit are absorbed in the rigours of abstinence, while those who love the world find their fortune ever on the advance."

Doulet Khaun, again, was the chief of the eunuchs of my father's seraglio, and obtained in this employment the title of Nazzir-ud-Doulah (regulator of the state). Of this man I will venture to say, that in the receipt of bribes, and his disregard of every principle of duty, there was not his second in the empire. In specie alone, he left at his death no less a sum than ten krour of ashrefies of five methkals,* exclusive of jewels, and gold and silver plate, china-ware, and utensils of brass and copper, to the value of three krour more; the whole of which became an accession to my father's treasury.

Zuffer Khaun is the son of Zeyne Khaun Koukah, on whom my father had bestowed a multiplicity of favours, and whom, as well as Khaun-e-Azzem, he regarded as a son, although the latter did rank far higher in his esteem than either. Zuffer Khaun is however a man of excellent understanding, and I have ever entertained from his zeal and ability the very highest expectations. He inherits indeed his father's acuteness. There are few that can stand a competition with him in rapidity of perception, which is such, that in a flight of pigeons he will at a single glance state their number, without making one either more or less. With all this he possesses considerable skill in the music of the Hindûs; and he is an incomparable soldier.

Among other objects which I accomplished about this period was the suppression of a tribe of robbers called Fehndiah, who had long infested the roads about Agrah, and whom getting into my power, I caused to be trampled to death by elephants.

Râi Durgah, a dignitary of seven hundred at my accession, and a man of the highest courage, signalized in many a conflict, although now far stricken in years, I advanced to the order of one thousand, bestowing upon him, at the same time, the donation of a lak of rupees. I also raised Mokheim Khaun, the son of Shûjayet Khaun, from the order of seven hundred to that of one thousand horse. The father, Shûjayet Khaun, was one of my father's most distinguished Ameirs; and I well remember receiving my father's orders, while yet a youth, to take my lessons

* Ninety krour of rupees, or ninety millions sterling!—utterly incredible.

lessons in archery under his tuition. Under these considerations I now made hima n Ameir of five thousand, with the insignia of the drum and standard.

A certain Roup Khawauss, after seducing from their duty one hundred and twenty of my father's slaves (qu. guards) had absconded; but was again taken at the discomfiture of Himmetpour. He was a man of the greatest courage, but an incorrigible drunkard. Add to this, he had never in the whole course of his life, once kept the fast of Ramzân nor uttered a prayer. For all this, I pardoned his guilt and spared his life.

Shahbauz Khaun again, although a fellow taken from the common bazar, an obscure market-man, nevertheless possessed the capacity of being extensively useful. Foul-mouthed and scurrilous as he was, even in the presence of my father, he received from him the first dignity of a grandee of five thousand. He understood, however, the Turkish language, and was well acquainted with the maxims of military discipline. Nevertheless, when front to front with the enemy, the terrors of the conflict were more than he could stand: I therefore removed him from the order of five thousand, and appointed him chief huntsman, with the rank of two hundred only.

Furthermore, to the different Munsebdaurs or functionaries, from the rank of five hundred downwards to the ohedy, or private horseman, such as are furnished with four horses each, I allotted to every one an augmentation of stipend according to circumstances of rank and merit. I also directed that thirty thousand of the ohedies should be always in attendance on the imperial stirrup, for the purpose of furnishing the nightly guards, in conformity with the established regulations of my court.

Mirza Shah Rokh, prince of Badakhshaun, the grandson of Mirza Sûliman, and my own relative, had attained under my father's authority to the rank of a commander of five thousand horse, and him I now advanced to the dignity of a grandee of the order of seven thousand, although somewhat at variance with the rule which dictated, that no Turk should rise beyond the rank of five thousand. Shah Rokh was a man of great simplicity of mind, highly esteemed by my father, who permitted to him, in common with his own sons, the indulgence of being seated in his presence. So much, indeed, did he partake in the simplicity natural to the Tartar race, that although he had lived in India for a period of twenty years, he could never accomplish the enunciation of one word in Hindûstauny. In the whole world, perhaps, there does not exist a race of men more notorious for their disregard of truth than the natives of Badakhshaun, although by no means deficient in intellect; but no one would have taken Shah Rokh for a Badakhshy, to whom he did not bear the slightest resemblance.

Notwithstanding the indulgence in which he had so largely partaken, it was

the

the misfortune of this prince, through the seduction of Meir Allâi-ud-deen the Badakhshanian, to incur the displeasure of my father, in consequence of which he had been sent towards Kabûl in custody of Khaujah Abdullah the Kabûlite. There happened at this period to be imprisoned in that city about four hundred individuals, taken in arms against their sovereign, and orders were despatched by the same opportunity, after proper admonition, and an oath never more to violate their allegiance, to set them at large, and conduct them to the metropolis of the empire. Without consulting Khaujah Abdullah, who was proceeding, as he well knew, to the same destination, this Allâi-ud-deen contrived to persuade the feudatories of the station that the instructions were to furnish these prisoners with arms and horses, and even with khelaats, and that he was employed to conduct them to the capital.

Unsuspicious of any perfidious design, the governor of Kabûl yielded to these insidious representations, and issued his warrant for the supply of the four hundred prisoners with arms and every necessary military equipment, as well as honorary dresses. On which these traitors, uniting themselves with Meir Allâi-ud-deen, before the governor could be made aware of their intentions, fell upon the city, and commenced an indiscriminate plunder of the bankers' shops and bazars, and with all they could lay hands on hastily withdrew through the city gates, and made the best of their way towards Badakhshaun. Nevertheless some years afterwards, although, after being admitted into the order of two thousand, he could thus absurdly as well as basely, and without the slightest grievance to complain of, violate his allegiance, when, after enduring every species of privation and wretchedness, he conveyed himself to my presence, and I demanded of him with what face he could venture to appear before me after such an act of perfidy and ingratitude towards my father, he replied in such terms of humiliation and contrition, that, notwithstanding such experience of his falsehood, I could not, in compassion to his misfortunes, withhold myself from restoring this Allâi-ud-deen to the appointments which he held under my father, and advancing him, moreover, from the order of two thousand to that of two thousand five hundred. In this I was supported by the opinion of my Ameir-ul-Oomra, who referring to this man's distinguished courage as a soldier, urged the danger and inexpediency of discarding him for ever for a single offence, taking into consideration that for such offence he had already been the victim of so much suffering.

I may here observe, that at the moment I am writing, there are enrolled in my service not less than one hundred and fifty thousand Ouzbek cavalry, from the rank or order of one hundred downwards to the private horseman. Nevertheless I am constrained to remark, that however brave in battle, they are very easily prevailed upon to desert their employers.

Some

Some time previous to my accession, I had conferred upon Sheikh Hussun Bulnâr the title of Mokurreb Khaun; and this person it was that I selected to proceed into the Dekkan to the camp of the Khaun Khanan, in order to bring away the children of my deceased brother Danial; for which purpose he received from me the best instructions I could devise, to be communicated to that minister. The commission thus entrusted to him, he finally executed with eminent ability, bringing away my brother's family and effects to a prodigious amount: the jewels alone being estimated at the value of nearly five krour of five methkaly ashrefies,* with two krour of the same currency in treasure.† He had at the same time two hundred elephants of the largest size, and nearly two thousand Persian horses in his stables. In justice I cannot omit to add, that as a servant the merit of Mokurreb Khaun is of the very highest order, and few are the sovereigns who possess his equal. In fine, I raised him to the dignity of an Ameir of five thousand horse, with the insignia of the great drum and standard, presenting him, at the same time, with a scimitar (shemsheir) set with diamonds, a charger with enriched caparison, a jewelled aigrette, a sumptuous honorary dress, and a trained elephant. It was on this occasion also that I conferred upon him the government of Gujerat.

Another whom I thought fit to elevate to the order of two thousand horse was Nekkeib Khaun, who bore originally the name of Ennayet-ul-Remly. He received his title of Nekkeib Khaun from my father, and was of the Seyeds of Kazvein. In other respects he was so extensively gifted in the knowledge of history, that however remote the points on which information was required, he gave it with as much facility as if consulted on the very spot, so unbounded were his powers of memory. He has completed seven volumes on historical subjects, and it must be confessed that in this branch of literature he is without a rival, and it might be justly said that of all creation there is no earthly monarch who possesses one like him. I shall lastly observe, that in early youth I studied for a short time under his tuition.‡

On the seventh day of the month of Shabaun (year not mentioned) Ramjee and Butcharam, and Seyam, the sons of Bugwandas, who was the uncle of Rajah Maun Sing, received the rewards of their perfidious deeds, having their heads crushed under the feet of my elephants, and being thus despatched to the hell prepared for them. Ramjee in particular was an idle and mischievous babbler, who

* Forty-five krour of rupees, or about £45,000,000 sterling!

† About £18,000,000 sterling, at nine rupees to the ashrefy. All these are sums so prodigious as to startle the most credulous.

‡ This is probably the same Nekkeib Khaun that translated the ancient Indian poem of the Mahabâret from Shanscrit into Persian, for he is also stated to have been a native of Kazvein.

who when his kinsman Pahar Sing, the son of Rajah Maun Sing, was raised to the order of two thousand at Allahabad, succeeded, with heartless officiousness, in persuading that unfortunate person to bring disgrace upon himself; and he was beginning to give effect to his malignant proceedings when he received the just compensation of his evil deeds.

Eiltcha Ram, another of the tribe, becoming alarmed at the execution of these men, was beginning also to exhibit some suspicious movements, with the same heartless indifference to consequences, when I consigned him to the custody of Mahommed Amein, the kroury (or collector) of Bengal, with injunctions to watch over him with the strictest vigilance. The father of Mahommed Amein, by the way, was one of the Seyeds Termed. He was instructed at the same time, that on his arrival in Bengal he was to place this man under the care of Rajah Maun Sing. With the greatest simplicity, after securing his hands and feet, this officer puts his prisoner into a common hackery, or covered bullock carriage, and thinking all sufficiently secure, proceeded with him, without any further precautions, on the way to Bengal. Between Serrâctaal and Ghazipour, about midnight one evening, when all were asleep, the prisoner watches his opportunity, and effects his escape, with the notorious design of joining the Rana. However, as this could not be accomplished without some noise, Mahommed Amein became apprised of the circumstance, and instantly proceeded in pursuit of the fugitive. The latter coming by accident to a part of the Jumnah where there was no ferry-boat, boldly plunges into the river, and gains the opposite bank in safety. But here his career terminates: he is laid hold of by some of the country people, and bound with ropes until the arrival of Mahommed Amein, to whom he is once more safely delivered up.

Mahommed Amein, upon this, transmits a despatch to my presence, announcing that he was again master of the person of his prisoner, whose design had been, as he alleged, to join the Rana, and requesting my further orders. I sent to acquaint him in reply, that if there were among the Hindûs of the Rajpout tribes any individuals willing to be his securities, I was disposed to pardon and give him a jaguir. Finding, however, probably from the notorious turbulence of his disposition, that no one would venture to become security for him, I consulted with the Ameir-ul-Oomra as to what, under such circumstances, ought to be done; for, if suffered to escape, such confusion might arise as it would be difficult to control, considering that the Rajpouts were in the country more numerous than cats and dogs. The Ameir-ul-Oomra stated, that to him there occurred only two alternatives, either to place him in the custody of some confidential individual, who would engage for his safe keeping, or at once to confine him in the fortress of Gualiar. Things came to this crisis, when Ibrauhim Gaugur,

gur, who had received the title of Dillawer Khaun, and Hausham Monguly, who had received that of Shahnowauz Khaun, both armed themselves, and putting their followers in order, prepared to rescue this Eiltcha Ram from the hands of Mahommed Amein, and carry him off to the enemy.

With these perplexing circumstances in mind, I secretly placed in readiness, in addition to those immediately about my person, a body of four thousand horse and two thousand touptchies, or matchlockmen, with orders, in case of any attempt against my personal security, to throw themselves upon the assailants, of whatever cast, and use their utmost efforts to prevent the rescue of Eiltcha Ram. Mahommed Amein was directed to keep fast his prisoner to the last extremity. In the interim Nowauzesh Khaun hastily entered, and announced to the Ameir-ul-Oomra that the rescue of Eiltcha had been actually effected, and that Mahommed Amein had been compelled to take post near the jeil, or lake, among the sebzah (green fields, or perhaps, grassy reeds) surrounding the lake. This report was communicated to me by the Ameir-ul-Oomra in a whisper. The tumult was now approaching with accumulated violence towards the foot of the royal tower of the castle of Agrah, and I intimated to the minister, that things appeared to have reached that crisis, beyond which it would be a crime to be longer idle. "Go then," said I, "with the soldiers under your orders, and render to these miscreants the reward of their treason." The Ameir-ul-Oomra accordingly led out his troops, and soon engaged with the insurgents. I next addressed myself to Sheikh Fereid the Bukhshy, observing to him, that I had not a doubt the insurgents would be immediately joined by all the Rajpouts in the neighbourhood, which would materially add to our danger; I therefore charged him to call out his followers, and hasten without delay to the support of the Ameir-ul-Oomra.

On the departure of Sheikh Fereid, the noise and tumult of the conflict became louder and louder, and I ascended to the upper works of the royal tower, where I gave audience to the people, and I thence observed the combatants hotly engaged; not less than twenty thousand of the Rajpout cavalry having joined the insurgents, and all of them now pressing furiously, sword and dagger in hand, upon the troops under the Ameir-ul-Oomra; while the latter, with all the skill of which he was master, was thus making head against the enemy. Kuttoub Khaun, one of the bravest and most useful of his retainers, together with many other gallant men, fell before my eyes by the swords of the insurgents, and a far greater number wounded. Dillawer Khaun,* who with others had charged the assailants to the assistance of Kuttoub Khaun, was dragged from his horse and sabred, all who accompanied him sharing the same fate. Joined by a reinforcement of three thousand

* There were two of these we must suppose.

thousand men, the which I dispatched to his support, the Ameer-ul-Oomra again bravely charged his assailants, and put a considerable number of the Rajpouts to the sword.

At such a moment, Sheikh Fereid, with ten thousand horse in quilted mail, and five thousand camel-mounted musqueteers, armed and in complete array, arrived to the support of the minister, and gave instant check to the fury of the Rajpouts. While the conflict thus continued with protracted violence, a single Rajpout approached sword in hand to make an attack upon Sheikh Fereid, who stood in advance under one of the standards. Seizing a javelin from one of his attendants, the sheikh passed it with such irresistible force through the breast of the Rajpout, that the point appeared clean at his back, which of course sent the miscreant on his way to hell. The superior prowess of the imperial troops was now apparent, and great numbers of the Rajpouts were put to the sword; those who escaped the slaughter betook themselves to flight in the utmost confusion. Of these, however, about four thousand were made prisoners, all of whom, as an example to other wretches who might be disposed to follow in their steps, were, by my command, trampled to death by elephants. At the same time, as a living example, to deter the turbulent and factious from engaging in such tortuous and disloyal designs, I directed the ringleader, whose name was Bukhta Ram, to be closely confined in the fortress of Gualiar.

It was on this occasion that Bahauder Khaun, an Ouzbek chief, ventured to make the remark, that if such an instance of rebellion had occurred under the authority of one of the sovereigns of his country, the whole tribe in all its branches would have been cut off from the face of the earth. To this I replied, that I could not forget, that from my father, in whose armies they served, these Rajpouts had received unbounded indulgence, and enjoyed distinctions far beyond their equals of other tribes; and, in consequence of the preference thus shewn them, it might have been that they were led to conceive themselves of a superior class. Neither could I consider it consistent with substantial justice, for the offence of a few misguided individuals, to extirpate a whole tribe, since, for every purpose of example, it was quite sufficient to punish the actually guilty.

I shall now return to the more grateful subject of recording the rewards and advancements bestowed upon the more faithful adherents of my government. I promoted Kauzy Abdullah the Kabûlite from the order of five hundred to that of five thousand; and on Khanjah Zakareia, the son of Khaujah Mahommed Yaheya, although in disgrace, I conferred the rank of five hundred. This I was induced to do on the recommendation of the venerated Sheikh Hûsseyne Jaumy, distinguished in our age for the unblemished purity of his life. Six months previous

vious to my accession, I had received an arrezdasht (or memorial) from the Sheikh, stating that he had recently had it revealed to him in a dream, that, to a moral certainty, the Most High would make me, in spite of all opposition, sovereign of Hindûstaun: on the occurrence of which event he should venture to solicit that for his sake, who had thus early predicted my exaltation, I would forgive the offences of the son of Khaujah Yaheya; and it was for this reason that I both pardoned and promoted the man.

On Taush Khaun Beg, also a native of the province of Kabûl, who had received from my father the title of Taush Khaun, leaving to him the same title, I conferred the rank of two thousand, presenting him at the same time with a richly caparisoned charger, jeigha and kreisse, both set with precious stones. This person is one of the oldest retainers of our house, having eminently distinguished himself as a soldier in the time of my grandfather Homayûn, and attained his rank of ameir under my uncle Mahommed Hakkeim Mirza. He is now far advanced in years, and, though his beard has lost its jetty blackness, yet retains his pleasing cast of features.

Another native of Kabûl whom I selected for promotion was Behajah Beg Khaun, whom I raised from the order of fifteen hundred to that of three thousand. This chief is a person of the greatest practical ability, and was reckoned amongt the most respectable of the ameirs in the train of Mohammed Hakkeim above mentioned. He is a man of distinguished courage, and though an ancient soldier, is a sincere Mussulman, rigidly strict in the observance of his religious duties. I shall here add, that within a very few days I have given preferment to nearly one hundred of the same tribe, with all the usual accompaniments.

Mirza Abul Kaussem, an ameir of one thousand, I advanced to the order of fifteen hundred. He also is one of my father's oldest retainers, a good soldier, and useful servant in other respects. It is remarkable, that of about thirty sons to whom he is the father, not one has turned to any good. It is, indeed, lamentable to observe, that the father of many sons but seldom derives any advantage from them in proportion to their number.

I conferred upon Sheikh Ally, the grandson of Sheikh Seleim of Adjmeir, the title of khaun, with the rank of an ameir of two thousand, presenting him at the same time with the sum of fifty thousand rupees, to celebrate the anniversary of his venerated relative. Sheikh Ally was bred up from infancy in the same apartments with myself, and is only one year my junior. He is a most intrepid soldier, and among the whole tribe has not now his equal. Strictly abstinent from inebriating drugs, or liquor of any kind, I entertain the highest expectations from his merit. In very truth it might be said, that I consider him as one of my own children.

G I bestowed

I bestowed upon Seyed 'Ally Assuf the titles of Seyf Khaun. He is of the Seyeds of Bâurah, and son of Seyed Mahmoud, who was one among the great Ameirs of my father's court, and a Seyed of the genuine stock. The son is worthy of his race, and no babbler. Than this, I do not know in man a better quality, and I despise the individual who is either rash in act, or hasty in discourse. In the whole course of his life I do not think that Seyf Khaun has ever been guilty of an unworthy action. He is also a stranger to inebriating drugs or spirits, and this very year I design to place him among the most exalted of nobles.

Next I promoted Feridoun, the son of Mahommed Kûly Khaun, from the order of one thousand to that of two thousand horse. Feridoun is the descendant of an illustrious race, and himself not deficient either in daring or generosity. His courage is such, indeed, that he is known to have been more than once engaged in conflict with a lion. This most formidable of wild beasts, with one hand wrapped in felt, and the other armed with a dagger, he contrived to overcome, by thrusting one hand into his jaws and stabbing him with the other until he killed him. To a Rajah Gahnum Pûll, the zemindaur of a purgunnah or district of the same name, with whom and his followers he was engaged in hostilities, he also opposed himself singly, and though wounded in several parts of his body, succeeded in keeping him in check until finally relieved.

I am now about to relate an occurrence, which from the struggle between private friendship and the sense of public duty, occasioned considerable pain to my mind. Mirza Nour, the son of Khaun-e-Auzem, was brought before me on a charge of homicide. This young man had possessed an extraordinary share in my father's friendship, was as much beloved by him as if he had been his own child, and who made considerable sacrifices to gratify and indulge him. In these circumstances, I directed that he should be taken, together with his accusers, immediately before the Kauzy and Meir-e-Auddel (or minister of justice), who received my injunctions, according to what might be proved in evidence, to fulfil with regard to him the dictates of the law. In due time a report was laid before me from these officers of justice, declaring that Mirza Nour, the son of Khaun-e-Auzem, had been found guilty of the wilful murder of a man, and that, according to the law of Mahommed, "blood alone was the compensation for blood." Notwithstanding my extreme regard for the son, and the respect which I bore for the father, I found it impossible to act in contravention to the ordinances of God, and I therefore, with whatever reluctance, consigned him to the hands of the executioner.

For a month afterwards, however, I endured for his death the most consuming grief, deeply regretting the loss of one so young, and possessed of so many elegant

elegant and engaging qualifications. But, however repugnant, there cannot in these cases be any alternative: for should we omit to discharge ourselves of this our irksome duty, every aggrieved person would seize his opportunity of time and place to avenge himself in his adversary's blood. To bring, therefore, to prompt punishment the man who violates the laws of his country, is an alternative with which no person intrusted with the reins of power is authorized to dispense.

[Here follow fourteen couplets, concluding with the remark, that the renown of Solomon, however exalted, is wholly derived from his inflexible love of justice.]

Informed of the execution of his son, but aware that there could be no evasion to elude the ordinances of God, Khaun-e-Auzem, after indulging in his grief for some days, finally suffered the melancholy occurrence to be banished from his mind. Of this distinguished Ameir I shall here observe, that he was an exquisite penman in the Nestaalik character, a very perfect reciter of the chapters of the Korân, and next to Nekkeib Khaun above-mentioned, I may venture to pronounce that he was unrivalled in the recollection of past events.

Like Khaun-e-Auzem, Assuf Khaun was also an excellent reciter of the Korân, an eloquent speaker, and without his equal in conviviality of disposition. In the whole court of my father there was not an Ameir more deservedly distinguished, and I myself continue to cherish for him the highest respect, of which I have given some proof in assigning to him the title of uncle. In truth, there are belonging to him such various accomplishments, both personal and intellectual, as can seldom fall to the lot of man. But there is one blemish clinging to his character sufficient to obliterate all his virtues: his hand is closed against the graces of liberality, than which there cannot be a deeper stain on the human character, more particularly in that of a man of his exalted rank; for the canker of avarice corrodes both here and hereafter. "I have exerted all the powers of reflection to decide, but there is no quality of the mind more graceful than liberality." Another fault by which he has exposed himself to censure, he was never known to pray. For this unpardonable defect he endeavours to apologize, by saying that he is prevented by the many temptations by which he is perpetually assailed. Neither has he ever been reclaimed, although with my father's permission he has made the voyage to Mekkah, and there performed the sacred ceremonies of the pilgrimage with every appearance of zeal and devotion; nevertheless, on rejoining my father in Hindûstaun, this neglect of his religious duties remained unabated.

I promoted Moezz-ul-moulk from the order of five hundred to that of one thousand. Originally he bore the name of Moezz-ud-Hûsseyne, and in my father's service had the superintendence of the goldsmith's department. I continued

tinued to him his title, with the appointment of diwan, or steward of my household (perhaps the director of buildings). Whatever in other respects might have been the ground of his claims, his singular simplicity of mind is a pledge of his love of truth, and he is moreover sufficiently ready with his pen. Sheikh Bayezzid, another grandson of Sheikh Seleim of Adjmeir, I raised from the rank of two thousand to that of three thousand horse. The first from whom I drew milk was the mother of Sheikh Bayezzid; and with regard to himself, such is his distinguished prudence, that place him in whatever employment you may, in his hands it cannot fail to prosper.

In conversation one evening with certain Pundits, the appellation by which their divines and learned men are distinguished by the Hindûs, I took occasion to demand, supposing it to be their intention, in the images which were the objects of their worship, in some sense or other to represent the nature or essence of the Deity, what could be a greater absurdity, or more revolting to the understanding, since we all knew that the Almighty is eternally exempt from change or decay, has neither length nor breadth, and must therefore be totally invisible; how then could it be possible to bring him in any shape under the imperfect scope of human vision? "If, on the other hand," continued I, "your idea is the descent or manifestation of the light divine in such bodies, we already know that the power of the divinity pervades all existence; this was announced to the legislator of Israel from the midst of the burning bush! If, again, it be your design to delineate by affinity (*qu.*) any of the attributes of the Supreme Being, we must confess that here below there cannot in reality exist any affinity, otherwise we might have expected some such manifestation by the hands of those whom, in any religion, we believe to have possessed the faculty of working miracles, and who surpassed all other men in knowledge, in power, and every human perfection. But if you consider these figures as the immediate objects of adoration, and as the source from which you may derive support and assistance in these designs, this is a most fearful conclusion, since adoration is due to God alone, supreme in glory, who has neither equal nor associate." After a variety of arguments for and against, the most intelligent of these Pundits seemed convinced of the weakness of their cause, finally confessing, once for all, that without the intervention of these images they found it impossible to settle their minds to a steady contemplation of the perfections of the Supreme Being. To which, in reply, I could only observe, in what manner, after all, was it that these images of theirs could contribute to the attainment of such an object.*

With these pundits my father Akbar was in the constant habit of familiar conversation

* I have endeavoured to give to this curious passage the corresponding ideas in English.

versation on every subject. He associated, indeed, with the learned among the Hindûs of every description; and although he might not have derived any particular advantage from the attainment, he had acquired such a knowledge of the elegance of composition, both in prose and verse, that a person not acquainted with the circumstances of his elevated character and station, might have set him down as profoundly learned in every branch of science.

I shall here consign to perpetual remembrance, that in person my father was tall in stature, of a ruddy, or wheaten, or nut-brown complexion; his eyes and eyebrows dark, the latter running across into each other. Handsome in his exterior, he had the strength of a lion, which was indicated by the extraordinary breadth of his chest, and the length of his arms. In the whole, at all events, his exterior was most captivating. A black mole which he had on his nose, was declared by those skilled in the science of physiognomy to prognosticate an extraordinary career of good fortune: neither could he, indeed, be considered very unfortunate, who sounded the great drum of sovereign power for a period of sixty-five years, and that over a part of Hindûstaun two years' journey in compass, without a rival and without an opponent.

To furnish some estimate of the prodigious amount to which his treasures had accumulated, I should state, that having one day given orders to Kilidge Khaun to bring him an account of the gold alone in the imperial depositories, that officer took measures as far as possible to ascertain what was to be found in the treasury at Agrah. He obtained from different tradesmen in the city four hundred pairs of scales, which for a period of five months he kept at work, both day and night, in weighing the coin and precious metals. At the end of that period my father sent to inquire how many maunns of gold had been brought to account. The reply was, that although for the whole of the five months a thousand men, with four hundred pair of scales, had been night and day unceasingly employed in weighing the contents of one only of the treasuries, they had not yet completed that part of their work. On which my father despatched to desire that matters might be left as they stood; to return the metals to their places, to secure them under lock and seal, and repair to the presence. This, it is to be observed, was the treasury of one cityonly.*

The establishment of elephants which he had formed never was and never will be equalled by any earthly sovereign, for it comes not within the limits of ordinary calculation that any one will be able to bring together *twelve thousand elephants* of the largest class (mungloussy), with no less than twenty thousand of another class (females), to provide forage and provender for them, incurring a daily

* This may probably be one among many exaggerations; but in gold and jewels this was doubtless the richest monarch the world ever saw.

a daily expense of four laks of rupees, equivalent to twelve thousand tomauns of Irâk.* His hunting establishment was of a corresponding magnitude. Among other animals he had twelve thousand one-eyed antelopes to serve for the chase; and of neilahgas, mountain rams, rhinoceroses, ostriches, and elout-e-derriai,† twelve thousand more.

For my part, I have discharged all the elephants, excepting those effectually trained for war, and a few more which I have retained for purposes of recreation. In conclusion, of the paraphernalia, the requisites for grandeur accumulated by my father, whether in treasure or splendid furniture of any description, the invincible Teymûr who subdued the world, and from whom my father was the eighth in descent, did not possess one-tenth part. But my father's footsteps were lofty, probably he was of an ambition to aspire beyond all that went before him. In the qualities of his mind he was indeed nothing a-kin to the denizens of this lower world.

When he arrived at the age of twenty, Providence bestowed upon him his first child, who received the name of Fautma Banú Begum, but died at the age of one year. Her mother was Beiby Pungrâi. By Beiby Araumbuksh he had two sons, one of whom received the name of Hussun, and the other Hûsseyne. The latter was given to nurse to Bereijah Begum, the mother of Assuf Khaun, but lived only eighteen days; the other was consigned to the care of Zeyne Khaun Koukah, and did not live the tenth day. After these he had by Beiby Seleima Begum a daughter whom he named Shahzâdah Khaunum, who was consigned to the care of his own mother, Mereiam Makauny (who has her place with Mary). Among all my sisters, in integrity, truth, and zeal for my welfare, she is without her equal; but her time is principally devoted to the worship of her Creator.

Next was born to him by Beiby Kheira a son, to whom they gave the name of Pahry. When he became of age, being employed by my father to conduct the operations in the Dekkan, he had reduced the fortresses of Gawil,‡ Parnalah, and other places of strength, and otherwise made successful progress towards the entire subjugation of the countries south of the Nerbudda. This prince died at Khaunpour in that territory at the early age of thirty. The name bestowed upon him by my father was Sûltan Mûrâd, but having been born among the hills of Futtahpour, and a hill in Hindûstauny being called pahr, my father in familiar language usually addressed him by the name of Pahry, or mountain-born.

* This would be about thirty-four rupees a day for every first-class elephant.

† I know not what animal this could have been, unless it was the hippopotamus; perhaps it was the sea-cow of, which they suspended the tails round their horses' necks.

† Gawuilgur, or Gur Gaweil. This place was captured in 1803 by Sir Arthur Wellesley.

born. In other respects Sûltan Mûrâd was of a greenish or fresh complexion, in person rather spare, and inclined to tall; in disposition mild, dignified, deliberate in council, and brave in action. In conduct so discreet, that my father consigned to him the superintendance of his building department and working establishments.

Subsequently my father had by Meher Semmaa a daughter, on whom he bestowed the name of Meeti Begum; meeti in Hindûstauny signifying sweet. She died, however, at eight months old. After this he had a son by Beeby Mereiom who was placed under the care of Râjah Baharmul.

Upon the death of Sûltan Mûrâd my brother Shahzadah Danial was sent to complete the subjugation of the Dekkan. On the arrival at Bûrhampour of my father, who was proceeding to the same destination, Sûltan Danial, accompanied by the Khaun Khanan and other distinguished ameirs of every class, with a formidable allotment of the imperial armies, was detached in advance; and it was at this period that the fortress of Ahmednuggur was reduced. My father came again to Bûrhampour, and having invested Sûltan Danial with the government of the Dekkan, returned to Agrah. Danial was not more than thirty years of age when he also died at Bûrhampour, in consequence of his intemperate indulgence in the use of spirituous liquors.

His death was accompanied with circumstances in some respects so remarkable, that I cannot withhold myself from recording them in this place.

He was extremely fond of shooting and the amusements of the chase, and had a favourite fowling-piece, to which he had given the name of jennauzah (the bier), and on which he had caused to be inlaid a couplet to the following purport:

> In the pleasures of the chase with thee, my soul breathes fresh and clear (tawzah),
> But who receives thy fatal mission, sinks lifeless on the bier (jennauzah).

His excesses in the disgraceful propensity to which I am compelled to refer, having been carried beyond all bounds of moderation, orders were at last issued, under the directions of Khaun Khanan, that he should no longer receive any supply of liquor, and that those who were detected in any attempt to convey such supply, would be punished with death. For some time, deterred by their fears of such punishment, none of his attendants ventured to utter even the names of liquors; and several days were permitted to elapse under these circumstances. At last, no longer able to endure this abstinence from his habitual indulgence, Danial, with tears and entreaties implored Mûrshed Kuly, one of his corps of gunners, to procure him even the most trifling quantity of the poisonous liquid, promising him advancement to the summit of his wishes provided he would comply with his request. Mûrshed Kûly, affected by the touching humility of the prince's prince's address, at last desired to know in what way it was possible to gratify him without incurring the risk of discovery and certain death. Danial replied, that at such a moment, a draught of liquor was to him as much as life itself.—"Go," said he, "and bring me the spirit in the barrel of one of my fowling pieces; twice or thrice repeated I shall be satisfied, and thou wilt be safe against discovery, or even suspicion." Subdued by these intreaties, Mûrshed Kûly did as he was desired; filled the piece so ominously named jennauzah with spirits, and brought it to his master. As the inauspicious name had been given to the piece by himself, it was so ordained by Providence that to drink what was conveyed by it and to be laid on his bier was one and the same thing—he drank of the liquid mischief and died: so true is it, that the tongue should be restrained from indulging in rash expressions.

In fine, what does not always occur in the same person, Danial was almost as fond of good eating as he was of drink. But there was one absurd ambition which seemed to be predominant with him beyond every other—that of possessing a superior train of elephants; to such a degree that, even among his own ameirs, if he saw one of surpassing size or quality, he did not scruple to take it away, sometimes forgetting the trifling ceremony of paying for it; of which hereafter. In short, as far as his power extended, he did not permit any one but himself to be master of a prime elephant. I shall lastly observe that Sûltan Danial was extremely fond of Hindûstauny music, and no bad reciter of Hindy poetry.

To return to the enumeration of my father's children, he had by Naun Beiby a daughter whom he named Lâla Begum, and whom he consigned also to the care of his mother, in whose charge she died at the expiration of eighteen months. Next, by Beiby Douletshah he had a daughter, on whom he bestowed the name of Araumbanu Begum. For this latter he entertained the greatest fondness, repeatedly recommending her to my protection, and charging me, for his sake, when he should be no more, to regard her with the same indulgent kindness—not without expressing his assurance, that his words would find a permanent place in my remembrance.

Of my father I may further observe, that in youth it would appear that he made good eating one of the greatest pleasures of his life, and considered a powerful appetite as one of its greatest blessings. Nevertheless, so sincere and humble a sense did he entertain of the superintending power of Providence, that, with armies so numerous and formidable at command, with a train of war elephants in number, and treasures in accumulation beyond all precedent, and an extent of empire, might, and grandeur never surpassed, he never for a moment permitted himself to be unmindful of that eternal Being whom he adored; and hence it was that the following couplet was ever on his lips: "Ever, in all places, with

with all men, and under every variety of circumstances, place thine eye and heart secretly inclined towards thine everlasting Friend."

But in his character one prominent feature was, that with every religion he seems to have entered, through life, into terms of unreserved concord, and with the virtuous and enlightened of every class, of every sect and profession of faith, he did not scruple to associate, as opportunities occurred; for the most part devoting the live-long night to this species of social enjoyment. And here it is to be remembered that, generally speaking, and taking the day and night together, his period of sleep did not extend in the whole to more than one pahar (or watch) of time..

His personal courage was of that fearless and imperturbable nature, that he has been seen not unfrequently to spring from the back of a female elephant to that of the most furious and refractory, known to have destroyed many a keeper, and this to the astonishment of those who had been most accustomed to the management of these enormous animals. On other occasions where the elephant was so furious and intractable as not to endure the approach of the female, he would ascend either a wall or a tree by which the elephant was to pass, and from thence cast himself without hesitation on the back of the infuriated animal; the mysterious energies with which the Almighty had endowed him being such that the elephant, as if by instinct of some supernatural influence, quietly submitted to his management.

In proof of his more than ordinary muscular powers, I shall relate, that he caused a massive iron chain to be made of ten Hindûstauny maunns, equal to an hundred maunns of Irâk in weight, which every morning he was in the habit of working about with such apparent facility as to be quite astonishing, it being an operation which required an uncommon degree of strength.

Of his extraordinary skill in military movements, indefatigable activity, and proficiency in the art of war, it will be sufficient to record the two following instances.

First. It is well known that when he ascended the throne of Hindûstaun, on the demise of my grandfather Hemayûn, my father was not more than fourteen years of age. It was at such a crisis that the infidel Himmû, who had made himself monarch of the Afghans, and to whom they pointed the finger as the hero of their tribe, put his armies in hostile array against the imperial authority. The conflict to which these indications of hostility led took place exactly on Thursday the sixth of Mohurrim, of the nine hundred and sixty-third of the Hidjera (20th of November, A.D. 1555). It is not surprising that this man should have been elated beyond measure with the contemplation of his power, when we reflect that he had been triumphant in two most sanguinary battles with the most puissant of Indian râjahs; that on this occasion he was at the head of

one

one hundred thousand horse, fifty thousand camel-mounted musqueteers, and three thousand elephants trained for the field; and that he should have borne, moreover, the reputation of being extremely brave in action. He sent, however, to my father a message, reminding him that, young as he was, he ought not to imagine that he was able to sustain a contest with a monarch of his superior might. "Come not," said he, "within the reach of my numerous and resistless troops and elephants, lest in the collision thou come to harm. I resign to thee all the territories eastward from the Jumnah to the uttermost limits of Bengal, and *mine* be the remainder of Hindûstaun." My father, in reply, desired him to reflect that there was little to boast of in his success over the unequal force of a petty Hindy chief—where was the renown of throwing a chain over his own slave? "Without experience of a battle with the brave, or having known aught of a shock with the warriors of my race, what canst thou conceive of the horrors of an equal conflict? The shadows of night disappear at the approach of day, when the Lord of Light unsheathes his sword of splendour. At to-morrow's dawn come to the field in thy strongest array, we shall then soon see whom God is disposed to favour."

Receiving this answer of defiance from my father, Himmû proceeded to communicate to his generals his arrangement for the battle, detaching a strong division with one thousand elephants in advance of the main body, and placing the remaining two thousand elephants in reserve in the rear of his line. In this disposition he presented himself at the head of his army and led them to the conflict. My father, on his part, having distributed his band of martial music upon elephants, and formed an advanced guard of five thousand mailed cavalry, with one thousand trained elephants, without further concern mounted his elephant and placed himself directly in front of Himmû. It is proper to state that my father's army consisted of no more than fifty thousand horse, and eight thousand camel-mounted gunners or matchlock-men. The battle commenced with a discharge of arrows and fire-arms, the elephants of the contending hosts being at the same time urged against each other by their keepers.

My father's fortune soon declared itself. An arrow transpierced the ill-fated Himmû through the head, and thus was he despatched to the abode of the wretched. His troops perceiving the catastrophe, immediately broke their ranks and fled: and thus were his boasted elephants, his treasures, and all the implements of his grandeur, at a single shift of fortune given to the winds. Shah Kûly Khaun Mohurrem, with some of his followers, happened to reach the spot where lay the throne of the fallen infidel, in the formation of which had been expended, in gold and jewels, the sum of two laks of five methkaly ashrefies;* and

* At nine rupees to the ashrefy, this would be eighteen laks of rupees, or £180,000 sterling.

and which, having with some difficulty saved from being pillaged, together with the elephant on which it had been mounted, he brought to the presence of my father. The mutilated head of Himmû, together with his tiara set with diamonds, sapphires, rubies, emeralds, and pearls, to the value of sixty laks of ashrefies,* was at the same time laid before my father.

This being his first victory, my father considered it an omen auspicious to the glory of his reign. In the exultation of the moment, he raised the fortunate Shah Kûly Khaun to the rank of an ameir of five thousand, with the insignia of the drum and standard. Treasure and valuable effects to an incredible amount, together with three thousand elephants, fifty thousand camels, and other articles too numerous for detail, were the immediate fruits of this triumphant day. On this occasion it was suggested to my father by his minister Beyram Khaun, to inflict a wound on the lifeless body, as a token of the consummation of his victory over the infidel. In reply my father observed, that sometime back, while amusing himself in his father's library, and looking at some paintings, the performance of Abdussummud the painter, a portrait was placed in his hands, which from the information of the attendants he found to be that of Himmû. "Instantly," said he, "I tore the thing to tatters, and threw it away from me. Let it suffice now that the man has met with his deserts; I considered that I had then achieved my victory over him."

When they came to count the slain in this battle, it was found that fourteen thousand of the infidels had been put to the sword, exclusive of those who escaped from the field and perished of their wounds.

[According to Abûl Fazzel this battle was fought, like most other battles for the sovereignty of Hindûstaun, in the vicinity of Pánipet, on Thursday the second of Mohurrim of the nine hundredth and sixty-fourth of the Hidjera, just one year later than described in the memoirs. The historian further states that Himmû, though pierced through the eye with an arrow, was yet alive when brought before Akbar, and obstinately refusing to speak, the young emperor, though urged to it, declined notwithstanding to pollute his sword with the blood of his defenceless captive; on which the minister Beyram Khaun put the unfortunate man to death with his own hand. With a feeling which reflects honour on his memory, Abûl Fazzel expresses his regret that the life of so brave and able a man should not have been spared, and his talents employed, as they might have been with perfect security, in the service of the state].

Secondly. Again, when information was brought to him at Futtahpour that the people of Gûjerat, under Mirza Ibrauhim Hûsseyne and Mirza Shah Mirza, had surrounded and laid siege to the city of Ahmedabad, although defended by

 a numerous

* Five krour and forty laks of rupees, or £5,400,000.

a numerous body of troops under Khaun-e-Auzem,* my father entered into consultation with some of his confidential servants, as to the measures to be adopted towards the punishment of these hostile proceedings. Beiby Begum, the mother of Khaun-e-Auzem, who was my father's nurse, was also present at this council by particular desire of my father. In concurrence with the suggestions of his faithful council, it was determined that a force should be immediately brought together, and my father proceeding in person at the head of his troops, the account with these redoubtable adversaries would be settled without much difficulty. It is to be observed, that from Futtahpour, where my father then held his court, to Gûjerat, is a distance of two months' journey. Nevertheless, having completed his equipments and put the troops in motion, my father by forced marches, which he continued night and day, sometimes on horseback and sometimes on a despatch camel, in fourteen days accomplished that which on ordinary occasions was a journey of two months, and placed himself in the very front of his enemies.

This was on a Wednesday in the second Jummaudy of the year nine hundred and eighty.† When close upon the insurgents, and not a vestige of the imperial garrison to be seen, it was in debate whether it would not be advisable to make a night attack upon the enemy. To this, however, my father objected, observing that these night attacks were the resource of the timid only, and suited those alone who proceeded by trick. At break of day therefore of the ensuing morning he directed the great drum for battle to be sounded, and a band of forty-five pair of kettle-drums and twenty Tatar horns striking up at once where they least expected it, produced the utmost astonishment in the camp of the enemy, whose attention had been hitherto entirely occupied with the siege of the opposite town.

Having mounted his horse and proceeded a little in advance, my father came to the right bank of the river Sâbermatty, and observing a body of the enemy on the opposite bank, gave instant orders that the troops should plunge into the stream in their present array, and at all hazards cross to the other side. He observed at the same time that the ground on the right bank was so overgrown with jungle, or brushwood, as to be most inconvenient for battle, and that if he allowed of any delay for the purpose of procuring boats, the enemy would rally their courage and become contumacious.

In these circumstances of surprise and alarm Mahommed Hûsseyne Mirza despatched some light troops to the river side, to demand of Sûbhaun Kûly, a Tûrkoman chief who had advanced to the opposite bank, what were the objects of this unlooked-for array, and who was the general who commanded? The Tûrkoman

* He was Akbar's foster-brother, therefore sometimes called Mirza Koukah.

† October, A.D. 1572.

Tûrkoman desired these equally ill-fated, and ignorant as they seemed to be, to be informed that the troops they saw before them were the advanced guard of the imperial armies, and that the emperor in person was present on the spot. Although their hearts had already begun to sink within them, and they could not yet divest themselves of their alarms, they ventured, however, to dispute the fact. "What absurdity is that you state!" said these mistaken men; "fourteen days ago only, our spies left the emperor at Futtahpour, and the army with its elephants and equipments could scarcely be conveyed hither in less than two months; this therefore must be a falsehood, and its authors could only be apostates and vagabonds escaped from the hands of justice."

My father now gave directions to place the troops in order of battle. Still there happened somewhat of delay; but the light troops bringing the report that the enemy were arming themselves, he finally gave the word to pass the river. At such a crisis, however, instead of obeying the orders conveyed to him to quit his ground, Khaun Kullan wrote to my father, to represent that the force of the enemy was great beyond all proportion of numbers; that the four greatest princes in Gûjerat were united at their head; that they had nearly two hundred thousand horse claid in mail or quilted coats, and twenty thousand camel-mounted matchlock-men, resolved to conquer or die; that they had moreover thirty thousand camel loads of rockets. That of all this he had, he said, undoubted intelligence. Until, therefore, the imperial army should have been joined by the troops under Khaun Khanan, Khaun-e-douraun, Khaun-e-jahaun, with the greater part of the expected reinforcements, it would be utterly repugnant to every maxim of prudence and discipline, with so small a body of men to cross the river, and place themselves in front of an enemy so very snperior.

To this my father replied, that he had ever, and on this occasion more than any other, reposed his confidence in the goodness of God, and in his never-failing support. That had his reliance been placed on human aid, he would never have committed himself thus almost alone to the presence of his mortal enemies. "The matter," said he, "is now in other hands. Whatever may be his will, must come to pass. But the enemy is advancing to give us battle, and it would be the height of absurdity, by any wavering or indecision on our part, to confirm and give him courage at such a moment."

Thus, although the cavalry and greater part of his principal generals were yet far in the rear, and those present did not amount to more than five thousand; although most of the Ameirs about his person urged the expediency of delay until the arrival of the main body to his support, my father resisted every importunity, and continued unshaken in his resolution to give battle. Just as matters were arrived at this perilous crisis, he suddenly dismounted from his horse, and

turning

turning his face towards the Keblah, or sanctuary of Makkah, humbly and earnestly besought the support of Him, who is the giver of victory and the author of all existence. Then remounting his charger, in perfect reliance on the aid of Providence, with the distinguished few who had the glorious destiny to be in attendance, he plunged fearlessly into the stream, and through the goodness of God, and the victorious fortune of his house, firmly established himself on the opposite bank; the whole of the companions of his glory on this occasion not amounting, when collected together, to more than five thousand horse. At this moment my father asked for his cloak (yelghah), which he had handed to Rajah Debchund, one of his attendants, to take care of, but which they now said had been lost or thrown away in the rapidity of the passage. "This," said my father, "is also an omen in our favour: the avenues to the field of battle will now be thrown more widely open; that is, we shall enter the conflict without incumbrance."

The imperial troops were by this time arriving in small parties on the river side, and plunging also into the stream, the body about the person of Akbar soon accumulated to ten thousand horse, together with one thousand elephants and two thousand gunners or matchlock-men. The refractory Mirzas, hurried to destruction by their destiny, continued all this time unmoved, at the head of a force so superior, ready for battle against their imperial master, for whose numerous acts of bounty and generosity they were making this ungrateful return.

Khaun-e-Auzem, who could not have conceived that his master had conveyed himself and his army to the spot with such astonishing celerity, now left the city and threw himself at his feet, swearing many an oath that he could yet scarcely believe the evidence of his senses. He was followed by Assuf Khaun and most of the other Ameirs of Ahmedabad, who successively hastened to present themselves to their sovereign.

All of a sudden, from among the trees of a neighbouring jungle, a body of the enemy made its appearance; and my father, with reliance unabated on his Maker, to whose providence he had resigned his cause, prepared with fortitude to receive the attack. Mahommed Kûly Khaun and Terkhan Diwaunah, with some others from the centre, made a movement forward; but suffering themselves to be repulsed by the enemy after a rather feeble attempt, my father expressed his displeasure, and addressing himself to Rajah Bugwandas,* briefly observed, that however superior the force of the enemy, which he confessed to be rather beyond what he could have wished, yet that they had no alternative but in their swords. "If," said he, "we but once shew our backs, the enemy will

* Of Ambér.

will derive courage from our cowardice, and not one of us will be suffered to escape. In full reliance on the power of the Creator we came to this spot, and be it our part, with one mind and one countenance, to make a concentrated effort against our adversaries : covered as they are with crimes and blood, the issue cannot be doubtful. It is with the clenched fist, not with the open hand, that our task is to be accomplished."

At this moment Mahommed Hûsseyne Mirza disengaged himself from the ranks of the enemy, and advanced to the front; observing which, Shah Kûly Khaun Mohurrem and Husseyne Khaun Tûrkoman called out that the crisis for a charge was arrived: to which my father cheerfully agreed. "I have secured for you," said he, "the aid of Providence, and the moment is arrived." They accordingly moved forward, but slowly and deliberately, until they came nearly in contact with their opponents.

My father was mounted on the occasion on a favourite charger, to which he had given the name of Kohpârah (montis pars), and which was repeatedly known to have rushed into the very jaws of an elephant. Clad in mail from head to foot, with lance in hand and quiver to his waist, and supported by the most distinguished heroes of his court, he now put himself in an attitude for the charge. The war band, composed of forty-five pairs of kettle-drums on elephants, with thirty horns and fifty trumpets, struck up at once, and the whole, to the cry of Allah-hû-Akbar, rushed sword in hand upon the enemy.

The terror which accompanied my father's renown, without any extraordinary effort, carried all before it on the left of the enemy; but the left wing of the imperial army having been repulsed by Mahommed Hûsseyne Mirza, that chief gained ground considerably on that side, and there stood embattled, in no little confidence of success. Some troops of the advanced guard, however, arriving on the spot, served for some time to keep him in check.

In these circumstances, my father being personally exposed to an incessant discharge of rockets from all quarters, it so happened that one of the rebel sirdars let off a rocket, which by accident taking the direction of one of their own elephants which carried a load of five hundred of these horrible implements of destruction, the whole immediately exploded, one after another, in the direction of their own ranks. These rockets striking at the same time among the other elephants and camels which carried the same destructive projectiles, to the number of a hundred thousand, all exploded in turn; and the elephants in their affright rushing upon their own army, the most tremendous confusion took place, nearly fifty thousand horses being either destroyed or dreadfully mutilated by the rockets. The effects of this fearful explosion were not less destructive among the men, and the whole immediately dispersing in

every

every direction, might be said, to all appearance, to have met with total annihilation.

My father, after proceeding a short distance in advance, suddenly checked his career, discreetly retaining in his hands the reins of strict discipline: while intent on observing the strange discomfiture which was at work among the enemy, who were flying in every direction, as if pursued by an hundred thousand warriors foaming with vengeance. In these circumstances, left with a few only of his personal retinue, my father was attacked by Mahommed Hûsseyne Mirza with his division, and for some time stood opposed to the most imminent personal danger. Maun Sing Derbaury, one of his attendants, combatted successfully in defence of his master; but Rajah Ragudas, another, was killed on the spot; while the faithful Woffadaur, a third, having received three wounds in his arm and hands, was borne from his horse, and compelled to combat on foot for the life of his benefactor.

Fortunately, the assailants seemed still unapprized that they were in presence of the emperor; and it was at such a crisis that three of the enemy's horsemen were seen making directly for his person. Two of these unaccountably turned aside, and passed on without attacking him; but the third continued to approach until close upon him. My father had seized a javelin from his armour-bearer, and was about to transfix him through the breast, when the man called for mercy, and declared that he came for the express purpose of announcing the splendid opportunity that lay before him; for that, panic-stricken by the exploding of the rockets, the enemy had neither strength nor courage for further resistance: and having thus delivered himself he rode away.

It was afterwards discovered that these three men had actually demanded to be employed against the person of the emperor, whom for some reward they had probably engaged to destroy. But approaching the spot where he fought, two of the assassins, appalled by the majesty of his presence, reined their horses the other way and withdrew: the third with greater boldness advanced close up to the emperor; but observing him couch his lance, and that death was otherwise inevitable, his only resource was to salute him with the annunciation of his victory, an expedient by which he contrived to escape with life.* My father continued to maintain the unequal conflict without shrinking, until the troops of the centre drawing near, gave positive information of the entire discomfiture and dispersion of the rebels. He then gave orders that the imperial troops should pursue to the utmost extremity, and not suffer a man to escape alive.

They

* According to Abûl Fazzel, who describes the conflict with great minuteness, all the three separately attacked the person of Akbar, and one of them actually cut him across the thigh; but that he escaped further harm by his singular address and activity, and the well managed movements of his charger.

They now began to collect the spoil, and nearly two thousand elephants, two thousand valuable Parthian horses (horses of Irâk) in mailed caparisons, and fifty thousand* dromedaries, with the small guns on their backs, were led to my father's presence. Shûjayet Khaun was foremost to congratulate him upon the magnitude of his victory, which could be ascribed alone, he said, to the interposition of Providence, with the influence, perhaps, of his own glorious destiny; for no one, he observed, could have calculated on the presence of the emperor so entirely unexpected, or that the defeat of an enemy's force so greatly superior should have been so strangely accomplished.

Having made his offering of praise and thanksgiving to the Dispenser of Victory, my father proceeded slowly towards the city of Ahmedabad, and while on his way thither, it was announced to him that Seyf Khaun Koukah had nobly fallen in the battle, and had departed to the mercy of his Creator. For a moment he became deeply affected by the report; but recovering his self-possession, he became sufficiently composed to listen to the particulars of his foster-brother's fate, who was the brother of Zeyne Khaun.

It is curious to relate, that some days previous to this battle of Ahmedabad, my father had given an entertainment to his Ameirs, at which were present a number of Shanahbein,† or blade-bone soothsayers, of whom he demanded, if their science enabled them to declare to whom, on the impending conflict, the victory would incline. They pronounced without hesitation, that the victory would be with him who was the object of homage, but that one of his most distinguished nobles would fall a martyr in the conflict. That same night Seyf Khaun expressed to my father his earnest hope that this destiny might be his alone, for he was come to die in the cause of his benefactor; and as he wished, so it came to pass. In the course of the battle, he had received two desperate wounds in the face, and he was hastening, covered with blood, to present himself to his sovereign, when intercepted by the division of the enemy under Mahommed Hûsseyne Mirza, he fell, sword in hand, fighting to the last gasp.

Mahommed Hûsseyne Mirza, who had usurped to himself the title and dignity of King of Gûjerat, was led, in his flight from the scene of discomfiture, through a grove or thicket of baubûl trees, the thorns of which being extremely sharp and strong, one of them pierced the foot of his horse, which fell, and the Mirza was constrained to continue his flight on foot. At this moment Gûddah Ally Beg, one of those who had the privilege of unreserved access to the presence of my father, overtook and secured the fugitive; so tying his hands behind, lest

 he

* More probably 5000.

† Literally *inspectors of blade-bone*, a sort of aruspices common in the East, who pretend to foretell events from the lines on the blade-bone of sheep: akin to divination by grounds of tea in the west.

he might attempt to escape, he placed him on horseback, and brought him to my father. Two other persons, however, claiming the merit of his capture, my father directed his prisoner to decide the point. "Alas!" replied the captive chief, "the emperor's salt has been my captor:" that is, the guilt of ingratitude for the bounty of my sovereign has led me into the snare. Moved with compassion at his sad reverse, however merited, my father directed that his hands should be unbound from behind, and secured before him. He was then consigned to the custody of Maun Sing Derbaury; but that chief, when he imploringly begged for a draught of water, ungenerously beating him with both hands about the head, my father interposed, and expressing his high displeasure, directed his attendants to relieve the unfortunate man from his own reserve. On this the Mirza seems to have intimated to his conqueror, that it would be advisable not yet to lay aside his precautions, for that, although one of the princes of Gûjerat had been defeated, and was his prisoner, there were three others still at large in the wilderness, who might yet occasion much trouble and alarm.

Slowly continuing his march towards the city, my father now transferred the care of Hûsseyne Mirza to Râi Sing,* whose daughter has at present a place in my domestic establishment, with orders to mount him, with his hands bound, on the back of an elephant, and so convey him into the town. While he was thus proceeding, another body of troops suddenly made its appearance in great force in the midst of the jungle, which although at the moment unknown, was afterwards discovered to be a division of Gûjerat, thirty thousand strong, under Èkhtiaur-ul-Moulk, one of the most powerful chiefs of the province, who now professed to be on his way to do homage at the feet of the emperor.

The imperial troops, naturally enough, becoming alarmed at this fresh display of a hostile force, my father ordered his martial music to strike up once more, and his warriors, mounted on fresh horses, again drew out for battle. In the mean time, Rajah Maun Sing,† Shûjayet Khaun, and Rajah Bugwandas,‡ with some light troops, advanced towards the strangers, and immediately commenced an attack; a volley of arrows, and a fire from nearly five thousand camel-guns, together with a simultaneous discharge of two thousand rockets, being directed at once upon the supposed enemy.

In this situation of affairs, Rajah Bugwandas sent a message to my father, reminding him that it was no longer safe to risk the escape of Mahommed Hûsseyne Mirza, and he therefore entreated his orders to strike off the rebel's head, as events seemed to have assumed an aspect of rather an alarming tendency. Such, however, was my father's compassionate disposition, that, notwithstanding the numerous proofs of ingratitude and perfidy on the part of the family, he could

* Rajah of Beekanair. † Heir-apparent of Ambér. ‡ Rajah of Ambér.

could not by any argument be prevailed upon to consent to this act of vengeance, however just. It was nevertheless carried to consummation without further ceremony, for the unfortunate Mirza, by a hint from Râi Sing, acting under the directions of Rajah Bugwandas, was suddenly thrown from the back of the elephant to the earth, and his head struck off by Sheir Mahommed.

But to return to Ekhtiaur-ul-Moulk. That chief, when he found it unavoidable, had dispatched a messenger to assure the emperor, that so far from any hostile design, he was come with no other intention, than of humbly testifying his loyalty at the foot of the throne. The imperial troops having, however, as we have seen, in the confusion of the sudden alarm, commenced the attack, the message could never be delivered, and he now applied his efforts to make his escape towards the hills. He was, however, soon pursued, and finally overtaken by Sohraub Beg the Tûrkomân, who, dismounting from his horse, immediately struck off his head.* Perceiving what had happened, his followers, at least such of them as were well mounted, fled in all directions, although ten thousand of them were thus unnecessarily put to the sword.

After this second victory on the same day, my father entered Ahmedabad without further accident. He remained here for the short period of seven days only; when leaving the province under the government of the Khaun Khanan, the son of Beyram Khaun, he returned to the metropolis.

It was subsequent to this, that the attention of my father was engaged in the conquest of Bengal, and the reduction of the impregnable fortresses of Chittore and Rintumpour, both of which latter undertakings he conducted in person. A chief of the name of Jeimul, who commanded the garrison of Chittore, while viewing the operations of the besiegers through one of the embrasures of the place, he shot through the head with his own hand; and the piece with which he exhibited this proof of his skill as a marksman, to which he gave the name of Droostandauz (*straightforward—never to miss*), is still in my possession. It must indeed have been a gun of matchless excellence, since my father is known, on good authority, to have killed with it, at different times, of birds and beasts not less than twenty thousand head; which is not less a proof of his singular skill than the goodness of the piece. I am myself not without some skill in the use of this weapon, being exceedingly fond of field sports of every kind, and having frequently with

 the

* According to Abûl Fazzel, Ekhtiaur-ul-Moulk had been left by the rebel Mirzas with his division to keep in check the numerous garrison of Ahmedabad, under Khaun-e-Auzem Mirza Koukah and Kotbuddem Khaun: but hearing of the defeat of his associates, and the capture of Mahommed Husseyne Mirza, he was making his retreat; and passing the right flank of the imperialists with about two hundred horse, while the main body was going round by the left, when being attacked in the manner described, he was compelled to fly.

the same piece killed twenty antelopes of a day. I made, however, a vow, that after attaining to the age of fifty, I would never more make use of a fowling-piece, and this was occasioned by the following extraordinary circumstance.

One day being engaged on a hunting party, among a herd of deer or antelopes which we had in view, I perceived one coloured and marked so beautifully, that I singled it out for my own pursuit, strictly forbidding any of my retinue from accompanying me, knowing, indeed, that the animal would be rendered wilder by the appearance of numbers. I discharged my piece, the same Droostandauz, at the creature repeatedly, without perceiving that my shot had any effect. As often as I closed upon the animal it bounded off, as if in entire derision. At last, after a third shot, I had once more approached close to the antelope, when givinga sudden spring, it in an instant disappeared altogether. Either from the sudden spring, or from some cause that I am unable to explain, I fell into a swoon, and remained in a state of total insensibility for the space of two hours; until, indeed, impatient at my non-appearance, my son Khoorum hastened to the spot in search of me, and applying rose-water to my temples, succeeded at last in restoring me to my faculties. I continued, however, in a state of debility and anxiety of mind for nearly a month; and from that day I solemnly vowed that, after attaining the age of fifty years, I would never make use of my gun in the chase.

Before I dismiss the subject of my royal father, I cannot omit to observe, that in the article of abstinence he was so far scrupulous, that for nearly three months in the year he never tasted animal food; but for the whole of the month in which he was born, he strictly forbid that any animal whatever should be deprived of life. It must however be acknowledged, that he did not keep the fast in the month of Ramzaun; but at the festival at the conclusion, he never failed to repair to the Eidgah, where he performed with due solemnity the double course of prayer, with all the other prescribed acts of devotion: and to compensate for his omission of the general fast, he bestowed their freedom upon three hundred slaves, and distributed fifty thousand rupees among the poor.

Among those who had been most closely attached to me during the period of my minority, was Jummaul-ud-dein Anjû, who had, indeed, in the time of my father, given the strongest proofs of devotion to my interests. He had hitherto held the rank of one thousand, but with the title of Ezz-ud-Dowlah, I now raised him to that of twelve thousand, a dignity never before conferred on any of the Ameirs of my father's court or my own. I bestowed upon him, at the same time, the insignia of the great drum and standard, a sword set with diamonds, a baldric similarly

* So named after his mother's tribe, the Khoorma or Cutchwa of Ambér.

similarly enriched, and a charger with embroidered and jewelled caparison. Thus did I accumulate upon him an hundred-fold the distinctions which he had held under my father's government, and still further aggrandized him by investing him with the government of Bahar, with the most ample powers for the exercise of his authority. And yet more, I conferred upon each of his eleven sons the rank of one or two thousand horse, according to circumstances: so that, among all the nobles of my court, none ever attained to such distinction, excepting alone the family of Ettemaud-ud-Dowlah, his children and relatives, to whose hands, indeed, have now been consigned all the cares of my government.

About this period my attention was engaged in regulating the currency of the empire, for which purpose I issued directions for a new coinage, the silver rupees and mohrs of gold in present circulation among the commercial and other classes having become in the course of time much debased or deteriorated, my object being to give to the new coinage an advantage over the old, and any difference unfavourable, to the new coinage being inadmissible. (Qu.)

Furthermore, having entrusted the funds destined for the support of the general poor to the superintendence of Meiran Sudder Jahaun, I consigned the management of the widows' fund on the same principle to Hadjy Koukah. About the same period I advanced Zauhid Khaun from the order of fifteen hundred to that of two thousand.

Another regulation which I considered it expedient to introduce about this period was the following: in the time of my father the superintendant of the present department, whenever it was thought fit to distinguish any person by the gift of a horse or elephant, the supply being always furnished from the imperial stables, was known to enjoy an annual profit to the amount of five laks of rupees,* equivalent to fifteen thousand tomauns of Irâk. This practice, which I considered equally absurd and oppressive, I caused to be abolished altogether; and I directed that henceforth the imperial bounty was not to be encumbered with any exaction in the shape of fee, perquisite, or emolument whatever.

It may be proper to mention here the arrival about this period of Sâlbahan from the Dekhan, with the property and effects of the departed Sûltan Danial, the middlemost of my brothers, which he now placed at my disposal. Among these may be enumerated fifteen hundred elephants of the largest class, each of which might be considered cheap at the price of four laks of rupees.† To these must be added eight thousand horses of the best breed of Irâk and Badakhshaun, none of less value than the other, and eight thousand road or despatch

* £50,000.

† £40.000 for a single elephant!

despatch camels. These were accompanied with all the appendages, all the requisites of a splendid court, with articles of gold brocade from China and elsewhere, the finest piece-goods of the manufacture of Gûjerat, and other commodities of the most valuable description. His jewels alone were estimated at fifty laks of ashrefies ;* the specie in his treasury amounted to six or eight laks more : the whole of which was now brought to account in my presence.

On the same occasion the three hundred women of my brother's harram were put under my protection. To these I caused it to be explained, that if any were desirous of being disposed of in marriage they were to make it known to me, and they would be betrothed to such of the retainers of my court as I might think fit. It is to be observed, that each of these females possessed a regular allotment of jewels, vestments of gold brocade, utensils of gold and silver, a canopied elephant and horses, as also a separate establishment of handsome eunuchs and beautiful female slaves, and last of all a dower or marriage portion of three laks of rupees ; all of which I freely relinquished to be conveyed with them to such of my Ameirs as they chose to espouse : thus at once relieving them from their constitutional wants, and myself from female importunity.

Among my brother's elephants devolved to me on the occasion was one of which I could not but express the greatest admiration, and to which I gave the name of Indraguj (*the elephant of India*). It was of a size I never before beheld: such as to get upon its back required a ladder of fourteen steps. It was of a disposition so gentle and tractable, that under its most furious excitements if an infant unwarily threw itself in its way, it would lay hold of it with its trunk and place it out of danger with the utmost care and tenderness. The animal was at the same time of such unparalelled speed and activity, that the fleetest horse was not able tokeep up with it, and such was its courage that it would attack with perfect readiness an hundred of the fiercest of its kind.

Such in other respects, although it may appear in some degree tedious to dwell upon the subject, were indeed the qualities of this noble and intelligent quadruped, that I assigned a band of music to attend upon it, and it was always preceded by a company of forty spearmen. It had for its beverage every morning a Hindustauny maunn of liquor, which is equal to ten maunns of Irâk ; and every morning and evening there were boiled for its meals four maunns of rice and two maunns of beef or mutton, with one maunn of oil, or clarified

* This at nine rupees to the ashrefy would amount to the sum of four krour and fifty laks of rupees, or £4,500,000.

clarified butter.* And this, it is to be remembered, although the elephants which descended to me on the demise of my father, alone amounted to twelve thousand, was the daily allowance allotted to each animal. From among all the others the same elephant was selected for my morning rides, and for this purpose there was always placed upon its back a throne or howdah of solid gold. Four maunns Hindustauny of gold was moreover wrought into rings, chains, and other ornaments, for its neck, breast, and legs: and lastly, its body was painted all over every day with the dust of sandal-wood.

It having been represented to me by certain individuals, that the departed Shah-zadah had, as formerly intimated, made use of force not only in the purchase of his elephants but of almost every other species of property, I caused it to be proclaimed, that if any of the persons thus aggrieved would come forward with their claims I was ready to make a restitution, in behalf of my brother, for any loss they might have sustained in their transactions with him.

I had in my possession a certain fowling-piece, for which I understood that Mirza Rustum had offered to the former owner the sum of twelve thousand rupees and ten horses, without success. As this appeared to me an extravagant consideration, I wrote to that person desiring to know what were the peculiar excellencies of the piece that could have induced such an offer. In reply he informed me, in the first place, that if fired a hundred times successively without intermission, the piece was never inconveniently heated; in the next place, that it was self-igniting, *i. e.* it was a firelock and not a matchlock; in the third, that a ball discharged from it never missed the mark; lastly, that it carried a ball of five mathkals weight. All these excellencies notwithstanding I made him a present of the gun.

On Saturday the seventeenth of Shavaul, of the year one thousaud and twenty,† I presented my son Khoorum‡ with a necklace of pearl and a diamond jeighah or aigrette, altogether of the value of eight laks of rupees.‖ In process of time, indeed, Khoorum became the proprietor of jewels to a very extraordinary amount. I only wish that in genius, and virtue, and every good quality, he may surpass all my other children in an equal degree.

On this same day I received from Kauzy Abdullah of Kabûl a written memorial representing the inconvenience and injury to the public revenue that would arise,

* Reckoning the maunn equal to 28 lbs., this would make about one hundred and ninety-six pounds weight per meal.

† 12th of December A.D. 1611, it was exactly the first day of the second month of the seventh year of his reign.

‡ Afterwards the Emperor Shahjahaun.

‖ £80,000.

arise, if my ordinance for the general remission of zekaat throughout the empire should extend to all descriptions of merchants, or such as thought proper to assume that character. It instantly occurred to me that this representation on the part of the worthy Kauzy had its origin, nevertheless, in views of sordid self-interest, and not, as he wished to make it appear, in zeal for the advancement of the revenue. I therefore issued a further decree, ordaining that whatever the question of merchant or no merchant, I peremptorily remitted the duties to all passengers conveying effects through the country without distinction. I caused it to be made known, moreover, that no person serving in my armies was to presume to transgress an order thus publicly repeated; and those employed to guard the passes into the country were charged, as they valued their heads, to beware, a thousand times over to beware, of making the collection of duty or any other object the pretext for oppressing the peaceeble traveller with exactions in any shape whatever.

Seyed Kamaul, the son of Seyed Abdulwahab the Bokharian, had been invested by my father with the government of Dehly, an appointment which he had been permitted to retain for a number of years. In the discharge of this important trust it now however appeared, that he had indulged in practices utterly inconsistent with that integrity which should ever distinguish the character of a just and upright government. For this it was at first my determination to bring him to condign punishment, the love of justice being the predominant principle in my nature. But recollecting the distinction which he enjoyed in my father's friendship, I was prevailed upon to forgive, without inflicting upon him any other penalty than suspension from his authority.

When I decreed the remission of zekaat (or tenths) throughout Hindustaun, the indulgence was extended to the province of Kabûl and its dependencies, of which latter altogether the revenue amounted in the time of my father to a krour of ashrefies.* Now the province of Kabûl may be considered to bear towards Hindustaun the same relation as Irân to Tûuraun. I was therefore desirous that the natives of Khorassaun and Ma-wer-un-Neher (Transoxiana) should enjoy the same advantages in the bounty of my government, in every respect, as the people of Hindustaun.

I had transferred the jaguir of Assof Khaun to Bauz Bahauder; but as the former stated that he had a claim on his jaguir for an arrear of two laks of rupees, I ordered the transfer to be suspended until such arrear should have been paid up. In the meantime, I directed that the sum of one lak of rupees should be immediately given to Assof Khaun from the imperial treasury, while Bauz Bahauder

* Nine krour of rupees, or £9,000,000.

hauder was enjoined to collect this arrear, and remit the whole to government:— about the same period, I conferred upon Sherreif Khaun the Afghan, who had accompanied my son Parveiz on the expedition against the Rânah of Oudipour, a donation of thirty thousand rupees. On the same day I bestowed the daughter of my great uncle, Hindal Mirza, upon Shah Kûly Khaun Mohurrem. She had been chosen by my father to take care of my son Khoorum.

On the evening of Sunday the eighth of Zilhudje, of the year one thousand and fourteen,* and at the expiration of the second watch of the night, it was that, misled by the counsels of evil-disposed and turbulent men, my son Khossrou became a fugitive from his father's presence, directing his views towards the territory of the Punjaub.

Soon after the hour just stated, the chiraghtchey, or lamp director of Khossrou's household, who was attached to the interests of Vezzeir-ul-Moulk, came and reported to that minister, that at the second watch of the night the Shahzâdah had left his quarter in the palace, and that the night-watch had expired without his re-appearance. Vezzeir-ul-Moulk conducted the man immediately to the Ameir-ul-Oomra, who had just quitted my presence and was on his way home, and to whom this extraordinary occurrence was now communicated. The Ameir-ul-Oomra repaired without delay to the palace, and having with some difficulty awakened the eunuchs in Khossrou's quarter, from them it was soon ascertained that the prince had actually absconded. A further delay of an hour and a half was consumed in making these necessary inquiries, and then the Ameir-ul-Oomra hastened to make known to me the circumstances of an event so extraordinary. I had retired for the night to the interior of my harram, and the minister had desired Khoujah Ekhlauss to inform me that he had something to communicate which demanded instant attention.

Conceiving that some intelligence had arrived either of disturbances in Gûjerat, which was ever the abode of turbulence and sedition, or of some hostile movements peradventure in the south of India, I joined the minister with no other expectation; when I received from him in detail all that he had been able to discover of the Shahzâdah's unaccountable disappearance. In my first surprise, I demanded in some perturbation what was best to be done; whether I should take horse in person, or despatch my son Khoorum in pursuit of the fugitive. The Ameir-ul-Oomra observed in reply, that if I would favour him with my commands, he entertained not a doubt but that, with God's assistance and the influence of my imperial fortune, he should be able to bring this untoward event

K to

* 31st of March, A.D. 1606. If this date be correct, the event which he is about to describe must have occurred about four months and eighteen days after his accession to the throne, and should have been introduced long since.

to a termination consistent with my wishes. He demanded, however, with considerable earnestness, what were my orders should matters come to an extremity, and the Shahzâdah appeal to the sword? I replied, that if he perceived that the affair could not be determined without a conflict, he was not to fail in the application of the resources placed at his disposal. In the concerns of sovereign power there is neither child nor kin. The alien who exerts himself in the cause of loyalty, is worth more than a thousand sons or kindred. He that employs his faculties to promote the interests of his benefactor, must command the utmost in the power of his sovereign to bestow. The son who in the presumption of his heart forgets the duty which he owes to his father, and the unnumbered marks of royal bounty so liberally bestowed, is to me, in every sense, a stranger. Though my son be considered the stability of the throne, yet when he betrays his hostile designs, he must be compared to the man who saps the foundation of his house and builds upon the upper story (terrace).

Again, the man who puts the seal to his ingratitude by an open demonstration of enmity, cannot expect that for him I should any more regard the claims of blood or proximity. Nay, have we not, in this respect, in Isslam a distinguished example laid, in the domestic policy of the monarchs of the house of Othman, who for the stability of their royal authority, *of all their sons preserve but one, considering it expedient to destroy all the rest.* What, then, if for the preservation of the state, if to prevent the disorders that might otherwise interrupt the peace of the world, I should think it necessary to extinguish the mischief, though it shew itself in the bosom of my own family? But independently of these considerations, I should have but little to boast of in capacity for the exercise of the power intrusted to me, if, after such a flagrant proof of his total disregard of filial duty, with my eyes open, I should ever again be tempted to intrust this wretched fugitive with the slightest share of authority. This would indeed be, with mine own hands to consign the power delegated by the Almighty supreme, to those ruinous contingencies to which the world would be exposed, from the baneful effects of profligacy and ignorance. I have never given countenance to an act of violence, even in a matter of the most trifling importance, how then can I pass it over in an affair of such vital consequence as that which now demands our exertions?

These reflections, suggested by a prudent concern for the general tranquillity, may perhaps be considered superfluous to a man of the Ameir-ul-Oomra's experience and discretion; but he seemed, on the occasion, to have sought advice from a principle of foresight, and more especially to give confidence and stability to men's minds. When he had, however, proceeded a short distance from my presence, it occurred to me, that although from long and intimate knowledge of

my

my person, his zeal and attachment stood above all question, yet at such a crisis this sudden departure from my presence might furnish to the evil-disposed and disaffected some suspicion against his loyalty; and I could not immediately divest myself of some uneasiness at the thought that his departure was in company with my son Khoorum, who was something younger than Khossrou. I need not observe, that with the generality of mankind the maxim is that the succession should rest in the eldest brother.

At the expiration of the third astronomical hour of the night, at all events, and not long after the Ameir-ul Oomra, whom I considered as a son, and who certainly enjoyed the most intimate share of my confidence, had taken to horse, I also felt myself irresistibly impelled to follow him.* In these circumstances I sent however to recall that minister, giving orders, at the same time, to Sheikh Fereid the Bukhshy to get in readiness all the troops that night on guard in the palace of Agrah. I also instructed Ehttemaum Khaun, who was kotwaul, or superintendant of police of the city, to despatch in every direction the most active messengers, announcing the event to the principal ameirs on the frontiers, and in every city and town through the empire, and requiring their immediate presence under the imperial standard. Those already on the spot received orders to be prepared to attend my person at the shortest notice.

The forty thousand long-tailed horses feeding in my stables were now brought forward, and as many as were required were immediately distributed among the most experienced and bravest of my guards and veterans, even to the number of one and two hundred each to many of the ameirs. I ordered out the whole of the swiftest road-camels of my establishment, to the number of one hundred thousand, and to every soldier who was not possessed of one fit for service was now given a fresh camel, with every other requisite equipment for the march. Every ameir and mûnsebdaur not immediately in attendance was at the same time directed to follow me without delay. Doust Mahommed and Mahommed Beg the Kabulite, whom I had recently dismissed for Kabûl and the Punjaub, and who had encamped some distance beyond Sekundera, now returned with the information that Shahzâdah Khossrou with thirty thousand followers had passed in that direction, and that he was marching with his utmost expedition towards the Punjaub.

After having distributed the fleetest horses and the swiftest going camels in my possession to every man whom I could trust, I mounted my horse; and as it seemed pretty well understood that the fugitive had taken the road to the left, I caused

* Here follow seven couplets, indicative of considerable distrust in mankind, which it would be tedious to insert, though by no means deficient in point.

caused every one whom we met to be examined on the subject, and all agreed that he was certainly proceeding towards the provinces on the Indus.

About daybreak I arrived at Sekundera, three kôsse from Agrah, where has been erected my father's mausoleum. Here Mirza Hussun, the son of Mirza Shah Rokh, who had been intercepted in attempting to join Shahzâdah Khossrou, was brought to my presence; and as he did not pretend to make any denial of the fact, I ordered him to be mounted on a camel with his hands tied behind him.

On this occasion, doubtless under the influence of my father's blessed spirit, an omen was displayed in my favour, which, however extraordinary it may appear, I cannot omit noticing in this place; and the more so, because it was something similar to what occurred at a remote period to my grandfather Homayûn. That prince, when about the age of fifteen, was on his way to visit the tomb of his father, the illustrious Bâber, and seeing a certain bird crossing his path, observed to his attendants, that if it were his destiny to succeed to the empire, the arrow which he was about to discharge would reach the bird at which he was taking aim. To his great delight the arrow passed right through the head of the bird, which fell dead at his feet. His conclusion was, that thenceforth, no design of any importance should be undertaken on his part without some such appeal to the decrees of destiny, since he had a firm persuasion that the accomplishment would infallibly correspond with the omen.

But to describe what took place in my own regard. I had mounted my horse on quitting my father's resting-place, and had not yet proceeded a kôsse on my march, when a man came to meet me who could not have possessed any knowledge of my person, and I demanded his name. He told me in answer that his name was Mûrad Khaujah. "Heaven be praised," said I, "my desire shall be attained." A little further on, and not far from the tomb of the Emperor Bâber, we met another man, driving before him an ass loaded with fire-wood, and having a burden of thorns on his own back. I asked of him the same information, and he told me to my great delight that his name was Dowlet Khaujah ('*sir fortune*'), and I expressed to those who were in attendance how encouraging it would be if the third person we met should bear the name of Saadet ('*auspicious*'). What then must have been the surprise when proceeding a little further on, on the bank of a rivulet to our right, and observing a little boy who was watching a cow grazing hard by, I ventured to ask him also his name; his answer was, my name is Saadet Khaujah ('*sir felix*'). A clamour of exultation arose among my attendants, and with feelings of equal gratitude and satisfaction, I from that moment determined that, in conformity with these three very auspicious prognostications,

tications, all the affairs of my government should be classed under three heads, to be called Eymaun-o-thalâtha ('*the three signs*').*

The second watch of the day had now expired, and the sun having attained the meridian, I was tempted to avail myself of the appearance of a shady tree to shelter myself against the scorching heat of the atmosphere. At this moment some melancholy reflexions passing through my mind, I could not forbear observing to Khaun-e-Auzem, that with all the accompaniments of imperial splendour, and the absence of all concern for the result, I was neverthelessexposed, and still more so were those who attended me, to many very serious inconveniences, against which we had not had the leisure sufficiently to provide; but what were these to the hardships endured by the unhappy boy who was flying under all the discouragements of guilt and dismay! Alas, what are our inconveniences to the sufferings in body and mind under which he labours? I confessed that my resentment was, however, not a little aggravated by the reflection that hostilities should have arisen at so early a period of my reign, and in such a quarter; that those who had shared for so many years in my toils and solicitude, should have thus exposed themselves to the inflictions of my just revenge. Nevertheless it afforded me some consolation that if I had not averted the imputation of neglect by taking horse at the instant, the wretched fugitive would by this time have gained some frontier ground, and there found himself joined by numbers of the factious and discontented—the perfidious hypocrites by whom he would have been soon surrounded. That I should personally engage in the enterprize was therefore without alternative, if I hoped to secure any reasonable prospect of success.

But to proceed with the narrative of this unnatural revolt. Arriving at a village remarkable for its numerous tanks and delightful groves, I determined there to encamp. It now appeared that when Khossrou reached Muttra, which is one of the most venerated places of Hindû worship (the Keblahgah, in fact), Hussun Beg the Badakhshanian entered the town with a body of his troops, and proceeded to exercise upon the defenceless inhabitants every species of violence and outrage; forcing from every one all the money they could lay hands on, and otherwise perpetrating such acts of profligacy and barbarity, that there remained no security for either sister, wife, or daughter in the whole neighbourhood. In short, such were the atrocities of every description of which these barbarians were guilty, that the unhappy Khossrou, not less alarmed than disgusted at the scenes of licentiousness and havoc of which he was thus compelled to

* If these circumstances did actually occur, and have not been put into the mouth of the imperial narrator by some ingenious fabulist, it must be confessed that they exhibit a very extraordinary coincidence, for the same facts are related, almost word for word, in the life of Homayûn.

to be a witness, broke forth among his attendants, in terms of agony and bitter self-reproach, to the following effect: "Alas," said he, "whither am I led, and from whom is it that I have been persuaded to separate myself? What is become of the glory which once surrounded my most ordinary enjoyments, that I should now be driven to address by the respected title of Ameir, those who have arisen from the very scum and dregs of society! That I should be compelled thus passively to look on at the enormities committed by such men on the subjects of my father's government!"

With these expressions upon his lips of repentance, self-reproach, and useless regret, suitable to the desperate lot to which he had abandoned himself, he nevertheless refrained, through folly and a false sense of shame, from recurring to the only remedy by which he could have been saved from ruin. For, as I stand in the presence of God, had the unhappy Khossrou, at this moment of returning shame and remorse, presented himself before me, not only would his offences have been overlooked, but his place in my esteem would have been higher than any thing he had previously enjoyed. Of this he had already experienced the strongest proof, when, after his unfilial conduct during the illness of my father, which I must have suspected to have arisen from hostile views and motives of the most dangerous nature, yet on his bare expression of repentance and a returning sense of duty, I freely banished from my mind every unfavourable impression. With regard to the circumstances of my father's last illness, and the means by which the duplicity and hostile designs of some turbulent ameirs became known to me on that occasion, I may remark that the influence of my predominant fortune was finally triumphant, and without the slightest effort of human skill God Almighty placed the empire of Hindûstaun at my disposal. The story and the events of which it furnishes the recital are among the extraordinary things of the age in which we live, and the particulars may be learnt with sufficient accuracy in the following relation.

On Monday the nineteenth of the former month of Jummaudy, of the year one thousand and fourteen,* during a paroxysm of his complaint, the inmates of my father's harram proposed to him, previous to his taking a particular draught (the *noush-e-jaun* or life draught) to eat of some fruit and other delicacies presented to him. The effect of this indulgence was a violent indigestion, and as his anger was at the same time to a violent degree excited against Amein-ud-dein, whom reproaching in severe terms for his gambling propensities, this combined with the previous malady, produced results so unfavourable, that the whole of the ensuing day was passed in complete abstinence, not a morsel passing his lips. This was on the Tuesday. On the next ensuing, which must have been Wednesday, they adminis-

* 16th of September, A.D. 1605.

administered to him the before-mentioned draught in some broth. Another day he spoke in terms of displeasure to Hakeem Ally, one of his physicians; who endeavoured to appease him [if it be possible to make common sense of the passage] by assuring him, that things done under the influence of alarm were always unavailing, and that his constant solicitude was the application of such remedies as were best calculated to relieve him.

My father, however, not less for the purpose of tranquillizing the alarm of his attendants than that of sustaining the remnant of life, consented to eat of some rue and vetches dressed with oil [the Indian dish called kithery, made of rue and dohl and eaten with ghee or clarified butter]. But such was the debilitated state of his bowels, that what he had eaten could not be digested, and a violent dysentery was the result. Hakeim Muzuffer, another of the physicians, now pronounced that his brother physician had grossly erred in his prescriptions, particularly in allowing melon to his patient, at the commencement of the attack. From a just repugnance to take away from any man his reputation, and perhaps from a disposition to forgive, I determined that Hakeim Ally should not be trodden under foot, at a mere malicious suggestion, or an accusation on the part of Mûzuffer actuated by mere jealousy. "If," thought I, "God's destiny and the blunders of the medical class did not sometimes concur, we should never die." This much, on a feeling of discretion and kindness, I confessed to Hakeim Ally; but on the bottom of my heart all confidence in his skill was extinguished.

During the last ten days of his illness, I attended my father as usual for two or three quarters of time in the latter part of the day; and this I continued to do until Tuesday the fourteenth of the latter Jummaudy, when he became so greatly reduced that I remained with him from the time at which his medicine was administered in the morning for the remaining part of the day. While he was yet in a state to discriminate, he advised me on one occasion to keep away from the palace; at all events, never to enter unattended by my own guards and retainers: and it now occurred to me that it would be prudent not to neglect such advice; that at such a crisis it behoved me in my intercourse with the palace to employ the most guarded circumspection. One day I entered the citadel accordingly attended by my own retinue. The very next day, without consulting their sovereign, they dared to close the gates of the citadel against me, and actually brought forward the ordnance on the towers.

On Thursday the sixteenth, perceiving the pretence of alarm under which these men were screening themselves, I discontinued my visit to the palace altogether; and I then received by Mokurreb Khaun, a note from Maun Sing expressing on his part the expectation that I would concur in their views. On this occasion I must in gratitude observe, that Mokurreb Khaun employed his oppor-

opportunities within the citadel with unceasing zeal and activity, and without allowing himself the ordinary intervals of repose, to promote my interests, and succeeded in a considerable degree in reclaiming the different Ameirs to a better sense of what was due to me. Of him I shall in this place also further observe, that holding already, under my father's government, the rank of an Ameir of two thousand, I repeatedly urged him to point out in what way I could be of further service to him; and when my father advanced me to the order of twelve thousand, the first of my own train that I made a mûnsebdaur, or dignitary, was Mokurreb Khaun, on whom, by an additional thousand, I then conferred the order of three thousand horse; but of his sincere and unabated zeal for my service I have ever experienced the very strongest proofs.

How deeply my feelings were agonized at the thoughts of being excluded from the sight of my father, during the period in which I thus abstained from entering the castle of Agrah, I for some time withheld myself from communicating to any man, resigning myself entirely to the will of God. There were, however, a few on whose discretion and experience I could rely, to whom I finally made known the circumstances of pain and grief by which I was oppressed. These were Meiran Sudderjahaun, Meir Rezza-ud-dein the Kazvinian, and Khaujah Weiss of Hamadaun.

These confidential friends took occasion to remind me of what had occurred to Shah Issmâil and Sûltan Hyder Mirza, on the very night of the death of Shah Tahmasp of Persia. Certain of the ameirs had, it seems, entered into a coalition for the sovereignty of Issmâil Mirza, who resided in the citadel of the metropolis; and on the night on which it was their turn to be on guard in the citadel, they entered into a consultation with the sister of Issmâil Mirza, to whom they communicated that there was a design on foot among some other ameirs to seize the persons of the adverse party, and to raise Hyder Mirza to the throne. That same night Shah Tahmasp expired; and Hûsseyne Beg with the ameirs who sought the elevation of Hyder Mirza, receiving the intelligence, brought his brother Mûstafa Mirza immediately against the place, and commenced a most furious assault. At last, conceiving the success of their resistance rather doubtful, the garrison of the citadel, to put an end to the dispute, struck off the head of Sûltan Hyder Mirza and threw it over the walls. Losing courage at the sight, Mûstafa Mirza immediately fled with ten thousand men in his train; by whom he was, however, soon abandoned, with the exception of Hûsseyne Beg and his brothers. But Mûstafa Mirza, not long afterwards, was seized by the same Hûsseyne Beg, and delivered to the new monarch Shah Issmâil, by whom he was finally put to death.

But to resume my particular narrative. Having with the advice of my truest friends

friends discontinued my visits to the castle, I sent my son Parveiz with an apology to my father, stating that I was prevented from attending upon him that day by a severe pain in my head. My father, lifting up his hands in prayer for my health, sent Khaujah Weissy to intreat that if possible I would come to his presence, for that he had no longer any hope of life, particularly under the violent paroxysms of his complaint. "Alas!" said he, "what a time is this that thou hast chosen to be absent from my person, when thou knowest that, on my demise, the succession to the crown is without dispute." Perceiving the crisis at which matters were arrived, the perfidious ameirs proceeded to swear the Mûssulmans on the Korân and the Hindûs on *salt*, that they had but one and the same language with themselves in their hypocritical design. Sheikh Fereid the Bokharian, who passed much of his time among these hypocrites, because with all his kindred he was in attendance upon the emperor, was in constant friendly communication with the faithful Mokurreb Khaun; while Mirza Koukah, usually entitled Khaun-e-Auzem, after the Mûssulmans and Hindûs had taken the oaths, sent a message to Shahzâdah Khossrou, my unduteous son, to congratulate him on his approaching elevation. But he desired to know whether father and son were of one mind and one language on the subject, that, as he said, he might not be rendered odious to, or disgraced by one or other of the parties. To these absurd and selfish speculations Khossrou sent for answer, that the succession having been secured to him beyond all question, all these scruples appeared to be quite superfluous.

Both Mirza Koukah and Khossrou thus equally assured, the latter suggested to Rajah Maun Sing, that as there remained in the emperor scarcely a spark of life, it was evident that he would not be able to bear the motion of the *sookpal*,* and that if he should happen to expire in the removal, a heavy responsibility would rest with some one or other of them: he must therefore caution him to be upon his guard, for that there was not the smallest necessity for conveying the sick monarch out of the castle of Agrah. The argument seemed to have convinced the Rajah: nevertheless, watching the moment when my father should recover from a fit of delirium, he ventured to propose, that as the whole body of the people collected under Shahzâdah Seleim (the memorialist) were besieging the castle, if it were his pleasure it might be as well to remove for a few days to the other side of the Jumnah; and the moment his health was restored, he might return again without obstacle to his palace. The sick monarch demanded, in reply, why this was come to pass? Surely they had not shut the gates of the castle in the face of the Shahzâdah, and thus been the cause of his drawing the troops together? With the assistance of some of his

 attendants,

* A litter: from *sook*, 'ease.'

attendants, the emperor turned to the other side on his bed, and Mirza Azziz Koukah, on whose brows be now for ever placed the blushing (rosy) chaplet of falsehood, observing his master reposing in that condition, entered the chamber, and making a sign with both hands, presumed to ask what were his majesty's commands with respect to Khossrou.

To this the sick monarch replied, "the decree is God's decree, and of him alone is the sovereignty. For my own part, with one mind I retain a thousand hopes. Surely, in giving a loose to such language in my presence, you have abandoned me to the jaws of death. Nevertheless it may happen that I have still some portion left in this life. If, however, the awful crisis be at hand—if the hour of departure be arrived, can I have forgotten the military promptitude, political sagacity, and other qualities indispensable to the successful exercise of sovereign power, which at Allahabad I witnessed in Seleim Shah? Neither do I find that the love and affection which I have ever borne him has for a moment been diminished. What if, through the misguidings of the evil one, he should for an instant have been led astray from his filial duty; is he not my eldest born, and, as such, the heir to my throne: to that throne which by the institutes of my race belongs to the eldest son, and never descends to him who is in years the younger? *But the six months' wide territory of Bengal I bestow upon Khossrou.*"

Having received these assurances from my father's lips, the specious hypocrites repaired in numerous groups to my presence, in such throngs, indeed, that the people had scarcely room to breathe. What, however, they thought necessary to communicate to me, they made known through Meiran Sudderjahaun Meir Jummaul-ud-dein Hûsseyne Anjû and Eidy Khaujah, and this was to the following effect: "The emperor, our sovereign, in giving to your son Khossrou every augmentation of rank, always instructed him to address your highness by the appellation of Shah-Bhye;* our prayer to your highness therefore is, that your treatment of your son shall be in every respect *paternal.*" My answer was, that in his conversation with me, my father never addressed me by any other name than that of bâba (child): it cannot, therefore, be denied, that on such occasions I was acknowledged as your future emperor; for the son can never be either brother or father.

By this answer the ameirs appeared to be involved in some perplexity, neither was it in their power to make any thing of a reasonable, much less a satisfactory reply. They seemed penitent of the part they had taken, and acknowledging their folly, cordially resolved on yielding to me, without further opposition, every proof of submission and allegiance; with the exception, however, of Mirza Koukah, who conveyed to me a second time his request for a private and confidential

* Brother prince. *Bhye* in Hindûstauny signifies brother.

dential interview. In answer, I sent to apprize him, that in consideration of many important services formerly rendered to my family, I had overlooked a long list of offences, some of them of considerable magnitude; and I had so overlooked them, because men sometimes expose themselves to the bitterness of remorse, without designing to offend. Would to God that I myself had no offence to answer for! "How often," said I, "have I not surrendered to thee the very inmost recesses of my heart, the repository, as far as thou wert concerned, of every kind feeling, liberality, and indulgence?" What more than this could he desire? Nevertheless, after so many proofs of my benevolence, if, in default of this interview, our intercourse was to cease, I consented to his request.

On Saturday, the eighteenth of the latter Jummaudy,* Sheikh Fereid the Bokharian came to do homage to me, and for thus anticipating his compeers in attention to my interests, he received from me the pre-eminent trust of principal functionary in all affairs, whether civil or military, together with the usual appendages of a scimitar, jeighah, and charger superbly caparisoned, together with one lak of rupees in specie. After him came Rajah Maun Sing, whom I also presented with an enriched kreisse and baldric, a horse and furniture, and otherwise treated with friendship and distinction. The day following Khossrou himself, accompanied by the same Rajah Maun Sing† and Mirza Azziz Koukah, was admitted to my presence; the latter urging me upon the request that the province of Bengal should be bestowed in full sovereignty upon Khossrou, and that Pâyendah Mahommed Teheghal should be sent to attend or assist him in his government.

Although it must be considered inconsistent with the ordinary maxims of policy to have allowed of the absence of Khossrou from my presence at the very commencement of my reign, obnoxious as he was to the suspicion of such ambitious views, and all about my person concurring in the opinion, I ventured, nevertheless, to comply with this request. I directed, at the same time, that they should embark and cross the Jumnah without entering the castle of Agrah, assuring them that as soon as the impending mournful event should have taken place, they would be permitted to proceed towards Bengal.

At this crisis of anxious suspence, my father sent me one of his dresses, with the turban taken from his own brows, and a message, importing that if I were reconciled to live without beholding the countenance of my father, that father, when I was absent, enjoyed neither peace nor repose. The moment I received the message, I clothed myself in the dress, and in humble duty proceeded into the castle. On Tuesday, the eighth of the month, my father drew his breath

 with

* Unless it was subsequent to the accession of Jahangueir, this must have been Saturday, the 5th. Akbar died on Wednesday, the 10th.

† The maternal uncle to Khossrou.

with great difficulty; and his dissolution being evidently at hand, he desired that I would despatch some one to summon every ameir, without exception, to his presence: "for I cannot endure," said he, "that any misunderstanding should subsist between you and those who for so many years have shared in my toil, and been the associates of my glory." Anxious to comply with his desire, I directed Khaujah Weissy to bring the whole of them to the dying monarch's sick chamber. Their names, were I separately to enumerate, would render our narrative unnecessarily tedious.

My father, after wistfully regarding them all round, intreated that they would bury in oblivion all the errors of which he could be justly accused,* and proceeded to address them in the following terms, arranged in couplets:

"Remember the repose and safety which blessed my reign,
The splendour and order which adorned my court, O remember.
Remember the crisis of my repentance, of my oft-revolving beads,
The canopy which I prepared for the sanctuary of the Kaabah.
Let the tear of affection shed rubies over my dust.
In your morning orisons turn your thoughts to my soul:
Let your evening invocations irradiate the gloom of night.
Do not forget the anguish of the tear-flowing eye.
When the chill winds shall visit your courts like the autumnal blast,
Think on that cold hand which has so often scattered gold among you."

He added the following stanza of four lines:

"Didst thou see how the sky shed around its flower-like fascinations?
My soul is on the wing to escape this cage of darkness.
That bosom, which the world was too narrow to contain,
Has scarcely space enough to inspire but half a breath."

Here I perceived that it might indeed be this mighty monarch's latest breath, and that the moment was arrived for discharging the last mournful duties of a son. In tears of anguish I approached his couch, and sobbing aloud, I placed my head at my father's feet. After I had then passed in solemn sorrow thrice round him, the dying monarch, as a sign auspicious to my fortune, beckoned to me to take his favourite scimitar futtah-ul-moulk,† and in his presence to gird it round my waist. Having so done, and again prostrated myself at his feet, I renewed my protestations of duty. So nearly was I indeed exhausted in these paroxysms of sorrow, that I found at last the utmost difficulty in drawing breath.

On the evening of Wednesday,‡ when one watch and four sections of the night were expired, my father's soul took flight to the realms above. He had, however,

* From the entire ignorance or negligence of the Persian transcriber, there has been considerable difficulty in reducing this passage into common sense.

† The conquest of empires.

‡ If the previous dates be at all correct, this must have been the 9th of the month.

however, previously desired me to send for Mêiran Sudderjahaun, in order to repeat with him the Kelmah shihaudet,* which he said it was his wish to postpone to the last moment, still cherishing the hope that the almighty Disposer of Life might yet bestow some prolongation. On his arrival, I placed Sudderjahaun on both knees by my father's side, and he commenced reciting the creed of the faithful. At this crisis my father desiring me to draw near, threw his arms about my neck, and addressed me in the following terms:

"My dear boy (bâba), take this my last farewell, for here we never meet again. Beware that thou dost not withdraw thy protecting regards from the secluded in my harram—that thou continue the same allowance for subsistence as was allotted by myself. Although my departure must cast a heavy burden upon thy mind, let not the words that are past be at once forgotten. Many a vow and many a covenant have been exchanged between us—break not the pledge which thou hast given me—forget it not. Beware! Many are the claims which I have upon thy soul. Be they great or be they small, do not thou forget them. Call to thy remembrance my deeds of martial glory. Forget not the exertions of that bounty which distributed so many a jewel. My servants and dependants, when I am gone, do not thou forget, nor the afflicted in the hour of need.—Ponder word for word on all that I have said—do thou bear all in mind; and again, forget me not."

After expressing himself as above, he directed Sudderjahaun once more to repeat the Kelmah, and he recited the solemn test himself with a voice equally loud and distinct. He then desired the Sudder to continue repeating by his pillow the Sourah neish, and another chapter of the Korân, together with the Adeilah prayer, in order that he might be enabled to render up his soul with as little struggle as possible. Accordingly Sudderjahaun had finished the Sourah neish, and had the last words of the prayer on his lips, when, with no other symptom than a tear-drop in the corner of his eye, my noble father resigned his soul into the hands of his Creator.

[Here follow thirteen couplets, of which we shall content ourselves with giving the sense of the four last.]

"That tall cypress, which was the glory of the garden, have they laid prostrate on the bed of desolation. Ever shifting world! who is exempt from the effect of thy fascinations? Rapid and undistinguishing in thy stroke, the noblest blood has no sparing from thee. From thy snares there is no escape. There is nothing certain but destiny—nothing adequate on the part of man, but resignation."

The venerated remains of my father were now laid on those boards, equally allotted

* The Mahommedan formula: "*There is no God but God,*" &c.

allotted to the prince and the pauper; whence, after being bathed in every description of perfume, camphor, musk, and roses, a shroud for his vestment, a coffin for his chamber, they were conveyed to their last repose. One foot of the bier was supported on my own shoulder, the three others by my three sons, until we passed the gates of the castle. Hence my sons, and the principal officers of my household, alternately bearing the coffin on their shoulders, proceeded all the way to Secundra, where all that was mortal of the renowned Akbar was consigned to the care of heaven's treasury. Thus it was, and thus it will be, while this lower world continues to exist.

Seated at the head of his hallowed grave, we mourned for seven days afterwards, observing in every particular the solemn rites of sepulture. I appointed especially twenty readers, to recite by his grave without ceasing, throughout the night, the sacred lessons of the Korân, and I immediately allotted five laks* of five-methkaly ashrefies for the erection of a lofty mausoleum over the tomb. During the seven days of our mourning, I also directed two hundred lungurs (or services) of food, and the same number of services of sweetmeats, to be distributed morning and evening to the poor who might attend. After this, the whole of the ameirs and other distinguished members of my court, who had accompanied in the solemnization of these funeral rites, returned to Agrah; and thus terminated the life of my rather, at the age of seventy-five years eleven months and nine days.

I shall here briefly repeat, that at the period of my father's death the greater part of the ameirs of the empire were combined in a plan adverse in every respect to my accession, and sought, by all the means in their power, to elevate my son Khossrou to the throne of Hindûstaun; designing, in fact, to leave to him the name only, while they retained to themselves the substantial exercise of the imperial authority. But the Supreme Disposer of events was on my side. The influence of the immaculate spirits of the imaums was in my favour. To the aid of no human exertion was I indebted for my crown; and a charge so momentous having been delegated to me by Him alone who knows neither change nor decay, I solemnly resolved, in my transactions with mankind, in the administration of justice, in protecting the defenceless, and in cherishing the poor and needy, to look to Him only to whom I owed my elevation, without the slightest regard to children or kin, or to any description of dependents whatever.

I have heard that one festival morning as he was quitting his bath, some one by accident threw a quantity of ashes on the head of Sheikh Bayezzid. Shaking the filth from his beard, and rubbing his hands across his chin, as if with a feeling of satisfaction, he exclaimed: "my soul, have I then been found thus worthy

* £450,000.

worthy—has this unlucky face of mine been worth a shower of ashes?—True greatness depends not either on reputation or report—elevation of mind belongs not either to the proud man or the boaster—humility will raise thy head above thine equals—pride will prostrate thee in the dust. The haughty and the arrogant behold head downwards—dost thou wish for distinction, seek it not."

I shall now return to the circumstances of the pursuit of the fugitive Khossrou. On Tuesday the tenth of Zilhudje,* we encamped at the station of Houdel, Sheikh Fereid the Bokharian still keeping in advance with a body of light cavalry. I was now induced to appoint Meir Moezz-ul-moulk, in consideration of his long and faithful attachment, to take charge of the important castle of Agrah, together with the treasure accumulated therein, in the room of Khaujah Jahaun. I gave orders at the same time that my sons who continued unshaken in fidelity should follow me without delay: for I had lost all confidence in years; and friendship and disunion had with me far greater weight than labour and fatigue, now that dire necessity had forced me into an absence of which I could not see the end, from my friends and all I loved.

On Thursday the twelfth of the same month our camp was at Feridabad, and on Friday the thirteenth † we reached Dehly, where I dismounted in the first instance at the tomb of my grandfather the Emperor Homayûn, doing homage to the immortal spirit of that illustrious monarch. I also gave to the surrounding poor the sum of thirty thousand rupees in alms, distributing both the money and pieces of cloth for vesture with my own hands. I proceeded thence to the grave of Sheikh Nizam-ud-dein Aoulia, intrusting the sum of fifty thousand rupees to Ameir Jamaul-ud-dein Anjû, and twenty thousand more to Hakeim Muzuffer, to be distributed among the indigent classes in the vicinity of the tomb. At this crisis I found it expedient to despatch orders to Ahmedabad, requiring that what was due upon the revenue of Gûjerat should be stated to Rajah Bikramajit; and the balance, after defraying the expenses of the youzbashies (or captains of fifties), specially accounted for to the imperial treasury.

On Saturday the fourteenth of Zilhudje my encampment was the caravanserai of Beirah, which had been burnt down and abandoned by the fugitive Khossrou. Here I advanced Aga Moulla from the class of one thousand and the quota of one hundred and fifty horse, to that of fifteen hundred; and I delivered to Jemeil Beg the Badakhshanian the sum of one lak of five-methkaly ashrefies,‡ to be divided among the men of his tribe, encouraging them at the same time with abundant hopes for the future: for these men were not yet quite at ease from their apprehensions, derived from recent refractory and rebellious proceedings. I further ordered for Rajah Maun Sing the sum of fifty thousand

* 2d of April, A.D. 1606. † 5th of April. ‡ Nine laks of rupees, or £90,000.

thousand rupees for distribution at Adjmeir, among the derveishes ministering round the resting-place of Mûeyen-ud-dein Chisti, and on Monday the sixteenth of the month we arrived at Pânipet.

This town has always been propitious to the fortune of the house of Teymûr, seeing that my father Akbar obtained two signal and decisive victories in the neighbourhood. The victory of my grandfather Homâyûn over Sûltan Ibrauhim Lody the Afghan, was also achieved on the plains of Pânipet. I shall here relate acircumstance which led to this latter victory.

Sekunder Lody, the son of Behlawel the Afghan and father of Ibrauhim, had appointed Doulet Khaun, the son of Tatar Khaun, governor of Pânipet, and the latter on the death of Sekunder Lody becoming the object of some jealousy and alarm to Ibrauhim, had been summoned to Dehly, the seat of government of the newly established monarch. But suspecting that there was some design in agitation that threatened his safety, Doulet Khaun contrived to evade the summons by delay, and sent his son Dillawer Khaun to appear in his stead. Finding this, Ibrauhim wrote to inform Dillawer, that if his father did not instantly appear at court he would infallibly be overtaken by the same punishment as had already befallen certain other refractory ameirs whom it was unnecessary to name. Dillawer Khaun did not fail to communicate this threatening message to his father; and the latter transmitting for answer that it did not exactly suit him to go to Dehly, immediately fled to Kabûl, where he joined the standard of my grandfather. It was in consideration of certain circumstances derived from this event that I raised Ibrauhim Khaun Gaugur to the highest rank and the title of Dillawey Khaun.*

However this may be, had Seyed Kamaul, the son of Seyed Hamid the Bokharian, been at Pânipet on the present occasion, instead of Dillawer Khaun, the unhappy Khossrou would never have succeeded in continuing his flight beyond that place: for so fatigued, harassed, and exhausted was he with hard riding and severe marches, and so discouraged his followers from the continual alarms of my rapid pursuit, that they were altogether in equal dismay and despair: add to this that my armies were closing round him on every side, in consequence of instructions early despatched by my orders. In the end, nevertheless, Dillawer Khaun Gaugur fully atoned for his error in quitting Pânipet, for hastening by forced marches to Lahour, he prevented that city from falling into the hands of Khossrou, as did Seyed Kamaul also in the subsequent action with Khossrou, as will be hereafter shewn.

At Pânipet, having been furnished with a litter,† through the assistance of the krouty,

* Ibrauhim Khaun was doubtless his original designation, as the son of Doulet Khaun.

† Singhaussin, a sort of dooly or palanquin.

kroury, or collector, Khossrou had been enabled to continue his flight, and Dillawer Khaun proceeding with his utmost expedition from the same place, failed not to apprize all he met with of the force that was approaching under the fugitive. Abdurraihman, the diwan, or chancellor, of the Punjaub, receiving from Dillawer Khaun intelligence of the approach of Khossrou, threw a garrison of eight thousand horse and foot into the castle of Lahour, and proceeded with a considerable body of troops to meet the fugitive prince, at whose feet however he immediately cast himself. For this act of treason and perfidy he received from Khossrou, with the title of Melek Anwar, the appointment of lieutenant-general under his ephemeral government. The perpetration of such a deed of atrocious ingratitude was however visited after the defeat of Khossrou with its just reward: for having been taken prisoner, I caused him to be sewed up in the raw skin of a black-coloured ass, and in that guise he was led about the streets and bazars of Lahour; until, through compassion for a numerous family of defenceless children, I prevailed upon myself to pardon his crimes and spare his life. For offences of this description there is, indeed, but little room for mercy; yet such is the tenderness of my disposition, there are few instances in which I do not rejoice at any sort of feasible plea for the exercise of this benevolent quality. There are, however, two offences in particular which those intrusted with the exercise of sovereign authority can never pardon: treason against the state, and treachery in the harram.

On Tuesday the seventeenth of Zilhudje, while at Karnaul, I conferred upon Aeid or Eidy Khaujah the rank of an ameir of two thousand, and I bestowed upon Sheikh Nozamm of Tahnaser the donation of six thousand rupees. Here it was communicated to me that an ordinary shop-keeper was going about persuading the people that he could shew them the Supreme Being in corporal substance, or in other words that he could exhibit the Creator to mortal vision;* and that he had contrived to impose upon vast numbers by his strange and impious discourses. Having failed in his attempt to seduce my understanding to the same absurd and impious speculation, I banished him from Hindustaun with permission to proceed to Mekkah.

On Thursday the nineteenth of the month,† we encamped at Shahabad, where we experienced the want of water to a very distressing degree. In prayer I lifted up my hands to heaven, and most providentially it so happened that on the self-same day there occurred a most copious fall of rain, which afforded to the assembled multitude which composed the army the most seasonable and abundant supply of that most valuable of blessings. A just estimate of the value of this most precious of the elements can indeed only be adequately formed in the midst of

* Perhaps a Roman Catholic exhibiting the *Host*.

† 11th of April, A.D. 1606.

of numerous armies; where instances have frequently occurred, in which men, who on ordinary occasions could scarcely be satisfied to drink of the crystal spring, have been known to swallow deep draughts impregnated with the most loathsome impurities, with as much satisfaction as if it were the very water of life. Nay, to the proudest monarchs on earth occasions have occurred, in which the weight in diamonds has been offered in vain for a draught of the precious beverage.

I can, in fact, adduce an instance in point which occurred immediately to myself, and it happened the first time in which I accompanied my father Akbar on one of his excursions into the valley of Kashmeir. Delighted with scenes of verdure and beauty not to be met with in the plains of Hindustaun, we had entered the mountain pass of Peirentehaul, when I lost sight of my attendants at a moment when I experienced the pressure of hunger in the extreme. In vain I sought for food or fruit, or drink—neither groom, nor cup-bearer, nor slave of any description was to be found in the midst of the multitude which thronged the narrow passes almost to suffocation.

I was, as I have said, labouring under the pressure of extreme hunger, and had made my way through the throng for a short distance, when I observed a few sheep which belonged to Assof Khaun. Instantly dismounting I seized one of the animals by the throat, and causing it to be slaughtered, desired that a kabaub (or fry) might be immediately prepared of the flesh, in order to allay the hunger which devoured me. At the moment I am writing these lines I am arrived at the age of forty years, and I can with truth declare that in the whole course of my life I never experienced such exquisite relish in food as in that simple meal, so opportunely furnished by this carcase of a stray sheep. I thus experienced what it was to be without the means at hand of appeasing hunger and allaying thirst; and my attendants were therefore instructed, whether on a march or on a hunting party, hereafter never to be without the case, canteri, or basket of refreshments. But while we remained in Kashmeir, neither the Khaun Khanan nor myself ever went unprovided with cakes of bread at least about our own persons. I cannot omit to mention that on this occasion it was stated by the Kashmirians that whenever blood was shed within the pass of Peirentehaul, whether of men or other animals, so that loss of life was the result, some awful convulsion of nature invariably ensued. I can only add that I never witnessed any thing that furnished the slightest confirmation of such a fact.

At the same encampment near Shahabad I conferred the office Meir Adil (or minister of justice) on Sheikh Ahmed Lahoury. He had held the same office under me previous to my accession, and I had never forgotten his services: and he had indeed received his education under my patronage; for of youths of this description,

description, whether as journalists, or otherwise employed, I had as my wards or disciples not less than sixty-six in number. All of these were instructed to be governed implicitly by certain rules of duty arranged for their observation. Of these we shall particularize the following:

In the disposal of their time they were never to be the dupes of their adversaries. Always to put their trust in the author of existence; always to commit themselves to the shield and protection of their Creator. Never with their own hands to be the death of any having life, excepting in the field of battle or the chase. Always to reverence the light as the abode of the glory and power of the Supreme Being. To consider all nature as bearing the impression of his Omnipotent Divinity. Always to keep in check the faculties of the mind. Never for a moment to be unmindful of God. In all undertakings to be governed by this impression—to do nothing without having him in remembrance.

In these maxims of mental discipline, my father, whose abode is now in paradise, and who in every thing has been my example and instructor, was pre-eminently perfect, making them ever the stedfast rules of his conduct, whether in his closet or his court. Neither am I myself less persuaded, that to have a sincere remembrance, and a just reliance on him who is the friend of all who serve him, is better than the professional sacrifices made in pretended devotion to him, while the imagination is intoxicated with the absurd vanities of this changeful world. Such, indeed, was the unwearied piety of that excellent prince, that I do not think the world ever furnished the example of its like; for from night to morning he was ever engaged, for the greater part, in meditation on the goodness of his Creator; in telling his praises by his revolving beads, and in prostrations before the throne of his eternal power. In his instructions, also, he never failed to inculcate, that if I were desirous of surmounting the difficulties of life, with ease to myself and satisfaction to others, I would neither rejoice nor place any reliance on any other than Him,* who is the cherishing principle of all creation. [The couplets are omitted which he describes as often repeated to him by his father.]

On Saturday the 21st of Zelhudje,† I encamped at the station of Anwund (or perhaps Anund), where I conferred upon Aeil Beg the Ouzbek the title of Bahauder Khaun, and thence despatched him with fifty-seven Ameirs and Mûnsebdaurs, from the order of one thousand to five thousand inclusive, to the support of Sheikh Fereid, who, with the advanced division, continued to precede us some distance in front. At the same time, I remitted to Sheikh Fereid the sum of

* One would scarcely credit that the man who recorded these sentiments was the same that employed his ruffians to murder the learned and enlightened Abûl Fazzel, and sent the intrepid Sheir Afkunn, the first husband of his wife, to perish, like Uriah, by the sword of the enemy.

† 13th April, 1606.

of ten laks of rupees,* equivalent to three thousand tomauns of Irâk, in order to defray his expenses in entertaining the same Bahauder Khaun, together with Jemmeil Beg the Badakhshanian, Shereif Ammole, and the other dignitaries; thus encouraging them, with an united object in view, to press vigorously upon the rebels, and accelerate those reports of success and victory which they were to transmit to my presence.

On the 24th of the month,† having obtained information that my triumphant banners had made their appearance in pursuit, certain of the most determined of Khossrou's generals received his permission to give battle. Sheikh Fereid on his part also bravely advanced his standard, at the foot of which he stood prepared for the attack. Bahauder Khaun above mentioned, to whom with my own hand I had devolved the sovereignty of Badakhshaun, and whom I knew to be a veteran and experienced soldier, proceeded to draw out his troops in order of battle; and having formed his army in three columns or divisions, with one of these he advanced directly upon the front of the enemy, while the two other divisions assailed them in flank. The action then commenced, and continued with sufficient obstinacy and considerable slaughter on both sides, until, of Khossrou's four principal generals, two betook themselves to flight, and the two others, with a thousand prisoners, were delivered alive into my hands. These I condemned to various punishments: some to be flayed alive, some to carry wooden yokes about their necks, others to be drawn through the river, and others to be trampled to death by my elephants. Those who escaped from the field wounded, conveyed themselves, heart-broken and harassed with dismay and terror, to the presence of Khossrou.

This same day reports repeatedly came in regarding the siege of the castle of Lahour, from which it became known that the garrison and the people of the town had embraced the same interest, and entered into engagements of mutual support. In these circumstances Hussun Beg Badakhshany represented to Khossrou that the people of Lahour were throwing open the doors of the imperial treasury, and were squandering the contents by extravagant donatives to the gunners who had made successful use of their pieces, independently of what was due to them as their regular pay; it being the design of this man, by persuading Khossrou to the pillage of Lahour, to involve him in irrevocable hostility, the city being indeed inhabited by men abounding in wealth and property of every description. Too easily misled by these insidious suggestions, and buoyed up by his expectations, that the plunder of the place would give him a treasury full to the skies, Khossrou gave instant orders that the gates should be closed; and the unhappy city was thus, for seven days, delivered up to ruthless and indiscriminate

* £100,000 sterling. † 16th of April.

minate pillage, the children of the wealthy inhabitants being seized on as hostages, and cast into prison.

The blood-stained banditti now set fire to one of the gates of the castle, which, it is here observed, together with the town is entered by twelve principal gates and four sally-ports. In the mean time Dillawer Khaun, with Hûsseyne Beg, who at present holds an employment in my household, Nour-ud-dein Kûly, the Kotwaul (or prefect of police), and others engaged in his support, hastened to defend the gate from within, the enemy not yet having succeeded in setting it on fire, the people from the inside incessantly pouring water upon it. By these means the wood-work of the gate being prevented from taking fire, the confidence of the enemy began to droop; and Nour-ud-dein Kûly, ascending the ramparts of the citadel, opened such a discharge of artillery and rockets from the walls and towers, as must have rendered the situation of the plunderers both hazardous and irksome in a very great degree.

The generals of Khossrou, not less than his troops, now despairing of the capture of the castle, and assailed by accumulating rumours of the approach of the imperial armies, began to perceive the folly of the treasons by which they had so deeply committed themselves; neither could they venture to foresee the moment at which, instead of laying siege to others, they should not be themselves besieged. All was now consternation, in which, nevertheless, setting their minds on battle and death, it was resolved, with one hundred and twelve thousand horse, which they had contrived to collect together, to make at night a bold and simultaneous attack upon my camp.

With this magnificent design in view, on Tuesday the 24th of Zilhudje, between the hours of evening prayer and supper-time, they abandoned the siege of the castle of Lahour, and withdrew from before the city altogether. On the evening of Thursday the 26th,* while at the serâi of Rhaujush Ally, intelligence was brought to me, that after raising the siege of Lahour, Khossrou, with about twenty thousand men, had gone off no one knew whither; and this awakening the greatest anxiety lest he might, after all, be able to elude my pursuit, I instantly gave orders to march, although there was at the time a heavy and incessant fall of rain. The same day I crossed the river of Goundwaul, and encamped at Dowaul.

It was on Thursday the 26th, about noon, that Sheikh Fereid succeeded in interrupting the march of Khossrou, and thus found himself at last in presence of the enemy. At this moment, at Sûltanpour, I had just seated myself, and was about to eat of some parched wheat, which was brought me by Moezz-ul-moulk, when intelligence was communicated to me of the situation of Sheikh Fereid, and

* 18th of April.

and that he was actually engaged with the troops of Khossrou. Having swallowed a single mouthful for good luck, I instantly called for and mounted my horse, and consigning myself entirely to the protection of God's providence, without suffering myself to be delayed by any concern for an array of battle, or being able to furnish myself at the moment with any other arms than my sword and a javelin, I gave the reins to my horse, and hastened towards the scene of the conflict. I had however about my person more than ten thousand horse, although none were apprised that they were that day to be led to battle. Neither was it indeed in strict conformity with the rules of military discipline, to engage in conflict with numbers so inferior, however favoured by Providence, the troops being, in fact, much disheartened by the contemplation of their manifest disparity. I endeavoured to remove these impressions, by directing the Bukhshies to order the whole army forward to our support without delay, and making generally known the crisis at which we were arrived. By the time I reached Goundwaul, accordingly, my force had amounted to twenty thousand horse and fifty thousand camel-mounted gunners or matchlockmen, all of whom I now forwarded to the support of Sheikh Fereid.

Things were at this perilous crisis when I thought it advisable to despatch Meir Jummaul-ud-dein Hûsseyne with a message to Khossrou, intreating that he would retrace his steps in time, and to beware of the awful responsibility to which he was exposing himself for the blood of such untold thousands of God's creatures. From this, though himself well-inclined to repair to my presence, he was however withheld by the counsels of the desperate and turbulent profligates by whom he was surrounded; and the reply which he conveyed to me through Jummaul-ud-dein imported, that having proceeded so far, there was no alternative but the sword; and that God Almighty would doubtless give the crown to that head which he knew to be most worthy of the empire.

When this presumptuous reply from Khossrou was communicated to me by Meir Jummaul-ud-dein, I sent to announce to Sheikh Fereid that there was no longer room for deliberation, and that he was at once to attack the main body of the rebels. These orders were carried into execution without a moment's delay. The attack commenced on one side from Bahauder Khaun the Ouzbek, at the head of thirty thousand horse in cotton mail, and twenty thousand camel-mounted matchlockmen; while Sheikh Fereid with a body-guard of chosen warriors rushed upon the enemy on the other. The army of Khossrou, on this occasion, consisted altogether of two hundred thousand horse and camel-mounted matchlockmen; the former clad in the same description of quilted mail as worn by the troops of Bahauder Khaun. The battle commenced at the close of the second watch of the day, and continued until sunset. The providence of God

God and the fortune of the empire being on my side, the result was a triumphant day for me: for when thirty thousand of the enemy had bitten the dust, the remainder discontinued all resistance and quitted the field in dismay.

Bahauder Khaun came, as it happened, to the very spot where Khossrou, having dismounted from his horse, had seated himself on a litter, conceiving that in the tumult and confusion of the pursuit he might possibly be able to escape without being known. Bahauder Khaun caused him however to be immediately surrounded by his troops, and Sheikh Fereid arriving also on the spot, Khossrou no longer perceiving the smallest outlet for escape, and that he must be overtaken without alternative, quitted the singhassun (or covered litter) on which he lay concealed, and announced to Sheikh Fereid that all further force was unnecessary, as he was, of his own accord, on the way to throw himself at his father's feet.

I call God to witness, that while at Goundwaul, at this perilous crisis, I experienced some strong forebodings that Khossrou was coming to my presence; but Jummaul-ud-dein Hûsseyne did not hesitate to express considerable doubt that Sheikh Fereid would that night be able to repulse the enemy, since, as he said, he had with his own eyes ascertained that Khossrou had with him a force of more than two hundred thousand fighting men. In this sort of discussion we were engaged when it was announced that Sheikh Fereid was victorious, and that Khossrou was his prisoner. Still incredulous of the joyful event, Jummaul-ud-dein dismounted from his horse, and throwing himself at my feet, persisted in the declaration, that although my imperial fortune indicated all that was propitious, still he could not yet give credit to the report. Every doubt was removed, however, a little afterwards, when Khossrou on his litter, accompanied by his general of artillery, was conducted into my presence.

Both Sheikh Fereid and Bahauder Khaun had conducted themselves on this trying occasion with distinguished ability and valour, and I immediately advanced the latter to the order of five thousaud, with the insignia of the drum and standard, and a present of horses with enriched caparisons, conferring upon him, moreover, the government of Kandahaur. Sheikh Fereid had previously possessed the rank of an Ameir of two thousand, and I now promoted him to that of four thousand. Seyf Khaun, the son of Seyed Mahmoud, had also greatly distinguished himself, having received not less than seventeen wounds in different parts of the body. Seyed Jullaul received a mortal wound in the upper region of the heart, of which he died a few days afterwards. He was of a distinguished family among the Afghans.

Seyed Hullaul and his brother, two of Khossrou's generals, terror-stricken by the din of the imperial kettle-drums, fled in consternation from the field at the very

very commencement of the action. Nearly four hundred heads of tribes, Owimauk, were sent to perdition in the conflict, and about seven hundred were brought from different quarters prisoners to my presence. The jewel-chest of Khossrou, containing jewels to the value of nearly two krour of five-methkaly ashrefies,* fell into the hands of some persons who were never discovered.

In the course of the same Thursday I entered the castle of Lahour, where I took up my abode in the royal pavilion built by my father on this principal tower, from which to view the combats of elephants. Seated in the pavilion, having directed a number of sharp stakes to be set up in the bed of the Rauvy, I caused the seven hundred traitors who had conspired with Khossrou against my authority to be impaled alive upon them. Than this there cannot exist a more excruciating punishment, since the wretches exposed frequently linger a long time in the most agonizing torture, before the hand of death relieves them; and the spectacle of such frightful agonies must, if any thing can, operate as a due example to deter others from similar acts of perfidy and treason towards their benefactors.

As the imperial treasury remained at Agrah, and it seemed inconsistent with good policy, in so early a stage of my authority, to continue long among the disaffected hypocrites at Lahour, I now quitted that place on my return to the metropolis, leaving the unhappy Khossrou a prey to the visitations of shame and remorse, in the custody of Dillawer Khaun, who had instructions to watch over him with unremitting vigilance. A son ought, indeed, always to be considered as the stay of monarchy; to continue therefore in a state of disunion and hostility with such would be to sap the foundations of its prosperity. Never have I permitted myself, either in this or any other instance, to be misled by injudicious counsels; my proceedings, as far as they were under my control, being ever governed by the dictates of my own reason and my own experience; constantly have I borne in mind the observation of that best of guides, my father, that there were two things of permanent utility to the sons of sovereign princes, prudence and fidelity in availing yourself of opportunities; the one indispensable to the preservation of sovereign power, and the other to the maintenance of a course of good fortune. But, too frequently, felicity in promoting a career of prosperity is found extremely inconstant; after a very limited period it slips through our fingers never to return.

But to resume the narrative. On the twenty-sixth of the month of Suffur, of the year one thousand and fifteen,† I returned to the metropolis of Agrah. I cannot omit to describe that, in sorrow for his past misconduct, the unhappy Khossrou

* Eighteen krour of rupees, or eighteen millions sterling, a sum too enormous for credibility.

† 15th of June, A.D. 1666, fifty Sundays after the battle with Khossrou.

Khossrou neither eat nor drank for the space of three days and three nights, which he consumed in tears and groans, hunger and thirst, and all those tokens of deep repentance, peculiar only to those on earth who have sustained the character of prophets and saints, but who have nevertheless found that a slight daily repast was still necessary to the support of life. It may be superfluous to remark, that an abstinence carried to the extremity of an entire fast for three days and three nights together, would inevitably have sent them on the fourth day to the bosom of mercy.*

[Of a certain Kalujen or Kumbujen, it is impossible to ascertain which, the imperial narrator proceeds to state as follows :]

In zeal, and diligence, and attention to the duties of his trust, he far surpassed his father. By night and by day he was unremitting in his attendance; wet or dry, rain or fair, leaning upon his staff, he would continue to read to me from night to morn. Neither did he discontinue his practice even when forming one of the suite on my hunting parties. For these services I had previous to my accession conferred upon him the order of one thousand horse, and I subsequently advanced him to that of two thousand. He is now, however, from his increasing corpulence, become in a great degree incapable of discharging the duties of his office with the activity which formerly distinguished him. I shall here remark, in passing, that kings do not look so much to the persons of men as to their services; and exactly in proportion as these latter improve in merit, so will be the advancement in favour, wealth, and dignity.

On the first day of every month, it was the rule with my father to set the example to his ameirs by discharging his musket, and this was followed by the whole train, from the highest dignitary to the lowest stipendiary enrolled in the service of the state, whether cannonier or matchlockman. But this discharge of artillery and musquetry never occurred but on that single occasion; unless, of course, in battle. In imitation of the same example I have continued the practice, a shot from my gun Droostandauz being followed by one from every individual in my armies, high or low. In short, the teffung, or matchlock-gun, is a weapon so unerring in its effects, has cost so much thought and skill in the invention, that an army preceded by fifty thousand camels, mounted by a force of this description, may be considered equal to the achievement of any undertaking whatever. I shall here further observe, that there are at present employed in the pay of the state, either immediately about my person, or that may be assembled at the very shortest notice, nearly five hundred thousand matchlockmen, either on foot or mounted on camels, independently of those engaged in defence

of

* The whole of this passage, from some omission on the part of the transcriber, it has been difficult to translate into common sense.

of the different fortresses, great cities, and other places, throughout the empire, which do not fall far short of thirty lacs, or three millions of men similarly armed; not including ordnance on the works of the numerous fortifications, some of which latter pieces require a charge of fifty and sixty maunns Hindûstauny of powder and ball.

At the period when I took my departure from Lahour for Agrah, on the occasion recently described, it happily occurred to me to direct that the different zemindaurs (or landholders) on that route, should plant at every town and village, and every stage and halting-place, all the way from Lahour to Agrah, mulberry, and other large and lofty trees affording shade, but particularly those with broad leaves and wide-spreading branches, in order that to all time to come the way-worn and weary traveller might find under their shadow repose and shelter from the scorching rays of the sun during the summer heats. I ordered, moreover, that spacious serrâis, choultries, or places of rest and refreshment, substantially built of brick or stone, so as to be secure against early decay, should be erected at the termination of every eight kôsse,* for the whole distance, all provided with baths, and to every one a tank or reservoir of fresh water: a certain number of attendants was also allotted to every serrâi, for the purpose of sweeping and keeping clean, and in other respects to take care of them. And, lastly, at the passage of every river, whether large or small, convenient bridges were erected, so that the industrious traveller might be enabled to pursue his objects without obstruction or delay.

In the same manner, all the way from Agrah to Bengal, a distance altogether of six months' journey, at similar intervals trees have been planted and serrâis erected, the former of which have already grown to such a size as to afford abundant shade. And more than this, many benevolent individuals, emulous of evincing their zeal in promoting my views, have at different stages laid out spacious gardens and plantations, containing every description of fruit tree; so that at the period at which I am writing, any one desirous of travelling to any quarter of my dominions, will find at convenient distances spacious buildings for his accommodation, and a refreshing supply of fruit and vegetables for his recreation; in so much, indeed, that he might be led to declare that he is a stranger to the fatigues of travelling.

Of a surety, these are the things of which the effects will be found beneficial both now and hereafter. Acts of this kind will sanctify our descent into the silent grave; will constitute our memorial in the world of the benefits derived from us to our fellow-creatures. *But with all this, we are not to exalt ourselves with the thought that the germ of vigilance is inherent in our nature, nor that faculty of*

* At one mile and a half to the kôsse, this would be at the end of every twelve miles.

*of foresight combined with humility in individuals of the stock of Adam, while the mind is so polluted with worldly gratifications, that not a methkal of gold or silver can be extracted for the purpose of being devoted to religious uses or the cause of God.**

With regard to the maxims which should govern the policy of sovereign princes, it has been said, that to resolve without the concurrence of men of experience is the most fallacious of proceedings; but I contend, nevertheless, that there is no safety in council, unless founded in rectitude of mind. I maintain, that if we intrust the concerns of the state to the opinions of another, we give to the Almighty an associate in the secrets of the heart. "We may pierce the sun itself with the diamond which points our vision; we may even penetrate the stars in their orbits by the same faculty; we may repose with safety in the jaws of the dragon; but we may not confide to any man the anxieties of the mind." He that conducts the destinies of his country by the judgment of another, must not forget that he will nevertheless be himself responsible, at the awful day of account, for all the exactions, the tyranny, the unjust decisions, violence, and oppression, to which the people may have been exposed, through such imprudent delegation. It is from the reigning sovereign that the awful reckoning will be required; not from those who have been his advisers. How much does it then behove the man who holds the crown and sceptre, in every clime, to make himself, by a personal investigation, immediately acquainted with the grievances of his people, so that assured redress may be always attainable, that no one should be within the grasp of oppression in any shape! I shall now recur to other matters.

Moussâheb Khaun, the Ouzbek, was distinguished for his bravery among the bravest of the age, and had attained, in the time of my father, to the rank of an ameir of three thousand. I now advanced him to the order of five thousand, assigning to him at the same time the foujdaury, or command of the armed force in Gûjerat. Some of the exploits of this intrepid man were worthy of the heroic Rûstum in the brightest periods of his career. The frontier districts of Gûjerat, previously an uncultivated and mountainous wilderness, overrun on every side with briars, thorn, and thistle, were under his management so cleared and improved, that a single person might traverse the country from one end to the other without difficulty or molestation. It was at the same period that he received from me the title of Khaun.

As an instance of the fearless courage and presence of mind of this brave soldier, I cannot forbear to relate, that on one occasion my father was engaged on

 a lion

* The passage in italics is so obscurely written in the Persian copy, that it has been impossible to give it any other sense than the above.

a lion hunt in the neighbourhood of Lahour, and had gone out attended by a body of four thousand matchlocks. Mounted on his elephant, he had entered the jungle or forest, which was known to be infested by these fierce and ferocious quadrupeds to the number of twenty, male and female. Most unexpectedly three of these, all females, at once attacked the elephant, and one of them making an astonishing spring, fastened on my father's thigh. Providentially Moussâheb Khaun, mounted on his horse Kohpârah (*montipars*), which feared neither lion nor elephant, came up at the moment, and instantly darting forward to the relief of his master, contrived to seize the lion by the back of the neck with one hand, while with the other he buried his khanjer, or knife, in the flank of the furious animal. Thus assailed, the latter fortunately quitted its hold without further injury. But this was not all; at the very crisis of peril the two lions together rushed upon Moussâheb Khaun, when, it will scarcely be thought credible, seizing both animals by the neck with either hand, he beat their heads together with such force that their brains issued from their mouths and nostrils. For these and other deeds of distinguished valour he has been most deservedly elevated to the title of Sereffrauz Khaun; neither is he less renowned for experience in war than for undaunted courage.

Another chief renowned for his courage was Mirza Mahmoud, of a distinguished family of Seyeds at Mûsh-hed, who possessed under my father the rank of five hundred, and whom I early promoted to that of an ameir of one thousand. It happened one day that a lion of enormous size, which had been wounded in a neighbouring forest by a musquet-shot, was brought to my presence, and lingered for some days before it finally expired. A doubt having been expressed by me whether it were possible with the single stroke of a scymitar to sever the head of this animal from the body, some of those in attendance seemed to agree that the thickness of the mane* at the back of the neck rendered this impossible. A certain Raujpout, however, who claimed relationship with Râjah Maun Sing, and remarkable for bodily strength as well as bravery, stepped forward and pledged himself, if I would give him permission, to strike off the head at a single stroke. Accordingly, drawing his sword, and with his utmost force making a stroke at the dead lion's neck, the only effect was the separation of a few hairs from the mane. Seeing this, Mirza Mahmoud approached, and also requested my permission to try his strength upon the lion's neck. "In the name of God," said I, "let us see what thou canst do." He accordingly advanced, and raising his sword on high, made it descend on the lion's neck with such force

* It has frequently been considered a matter of doubt whether the animal so often referred to under the denomination of *sheir* in these countries was not a tiger; but the circumstance of the mane sets the matter at rest, and hundreds of lions have been killed by our countrymen about Hisar.

force and skill that the head flew off to a considerable distance, exciting the clamorous applause of the whole assembly. I made him on the spot a present of thirty thousand rupees, and conferred upon him the title of Mirza Mahmoud Sheir-be-dou-neim (the lion-halver).

On another occasion a bow of remarkable excellence had been sent to me from Gujerat by Mirza Shumsy, the son of Mirza Koukah my father's foster-brother, which the strongest men had been unable to bend with the utmost exertion of bodily strength. The same Mirza Mahmoud again besought, and having obtained my permission to try his skill, took up the bow, and with little apparent difficulty brought the horns so far round as nearly to snap it in the middle, and this to the surprise of the bystanders. This afforded me another opportunity for the exertion of my bounty, and I advanced him from the order of one thousand to that of fifteen hundred, with the new title of Mirza Mahmoud Peitch-kemmaun (the bow-bender). Having subsequently received from me the appointment of foujdaur (or lord marcher) on the frontiers of Lahour, he became engaged in hostilities with a powerful Râjah in that quarter, whom he finally subjugated; and I then presented him with one of my finest elephants, with the title of Tehower Khaun, bestowing upon him at the same time in wedlock one of the female inmates of my own imperial palace.

Another of the ameirs of my court distinguished for courage and skill was Bauker Noodjum Thauni, who had not in the world his equal in the use of the bow. As an instance of the surprising perfection to which he had carried his practice it will be sufficient to relate, that one evening in my presence they placed before him a transparent glass bottle, or vessel of some kind or other, a torch or flambeaux being held at some distance behind the vessel; they then made of wax something in the shape of a fly, which they fixed to the side of the bottle, which was of the most delicate fabric: on the top of this piece of wax they set a grain of rice and a peppercorn. His first arrow struck the peppercorn, his second carried off the grain of rice, and the third struck the diminutive wax figure, without in the slightest degree touching or injuring the glass vessel, which was, as I have before observed, of the very lightest and most delicate material. This was a degree of skill in the bowman's art* amazing beyond all amazement; and it might be safely alleged that such an instance of perfection in the craft has never been exhibited in any age or nation. As a proof of my admiration I immediately advanced him from the order of one thousand to that of two thousand horse; and I bestowed upon him, moreover, under a contract of marriage, the

* Before we arrive at the sequel I think it will be acknowledged, that our imperial archer was himself the *boldest bowman* in all his dominions.

the sister's daughter of Nourjahaun Begum, in consequence of which union he became to me as a son of my own.

It had been made known to me that the roads about Kandahar were grievously infested by the Afghans, who by their vexatious exactions rendered the communications in that quarter extremely unsafe for travellers of every description. I had it therefore in contemplation to employ a competent force for the extirpation of these lawless marauders. But while I was yet deliberating on the subject, an individual of the nation of distinguished eminence in his tribe, and who now enjoys in my court the title of Allahdaud Khaun, communicated to me such convincing reasons, that I determined to appoint an imperial foujdaur for the province, under whose management, should they again set at nought the imperial authority, they might then be exterminated without further caution. I did not hesitate to vest the appointment in himself, and he still retains the office under my authority.

Another arrangement in the same quarter was not accomplished with quite as little difficulty. Lushker Khaun, who originally bore the name of Khaujah Abûl Hussun, and who had from an early period been attached to the service of the house of Teymûr, had recently been dignified with his title, and was despatched by my orders towards Kabûl for the purpose of clearing the roads in that direction, which had been also rendered unsafe by the outrages of a licentious banditti. It so happened that when this commander had nearly reached the point for which he was destined he found opposed to him a body of mountaineers, in manners and intellect not much better than wild beasts or devils, who had assembled to the number of forty thousand, horse and foot and matchlockmen, had shut up the approaches against him, and prevented his further advance. Confiding, nevertheless, in the goodness of God and my unwaning fortune, he did not hesitate, with whatever disparity of force, to precipitate himself upon such superior numbers. A conflict thus commenced, which continued with unabated obstinacy from dawn of day until nearly sunset. The enemy were however finally defeated, with the loss of seventeen thousand killed, a number taken prisoners, and a still greater proportion escaping to their hiding-places among the mountains. The prisoners were conducted to my presence yoked together, with the heads of the seventeen thousand slain in the battle suspended from their necks. *After some deliberation as to the destiny of these captives, I resolved that their lives should be spared, and that they should be employed in bringing forage for my elephants.**

The

* The passage in italics has been rendered for the most part by conjecture, the original being so completely unintelligible as to bid defiance to all research. From the words Nerd bakhteny, it might be conceived that the fate of these captives was decided by lot.

The intercourse with Kabûl, so long interrupted by the atrocities of these robbers, was now by the effect of Lushker Khaun's victory completely re-established, and the communication so well secured, that every description of fruit the produce of that province may at present be procured at Lahour every other day, although neither very cheap nor in great abundance. The shedding of so much human blood must ever be extremely painful; but until some other resource is discovered, it is unavoidable. Unhappily the functions of government cannot be carried on without severity, and occasional extinction of human life: for without something of the kind, some species of coercion and chastisement, the world would soon exhibit the horrible spectacle of mankind, like wild beasts, worrying each other to death with no other motive than rapacity and revenge. *God* is witness that there is no repose for crowned heads. There is no pain or anxiety equal to that which attends the possession of sovereign power, for to the possessor there is not in this world a moment's rest. Care and anxiety must ever be the lot of kings, for of an instant's inattention to the duties of their trust a thousand evils may be the result. Even sleep itself furnishes no repose for monarchs, the adversary being ever at work for the accomplishment of his designs. It has indeed been said that kings will find enemies in the very hair of their own bodies. "Let this my counsel be suspended like a jewel to thine ear. Hath heaven deposited in thine hands the power supreme—keep always well with the people subject to thy sway. Better that a man leave behind him a good name, than to leave behind him a palace of burnished gold."

While I am upon the subject, I cannot but consider that he to whom God hath assigned the pomp and splendour of imperial power, with a sacred and awful character in the eyes of his creatures, must, as he hopes for stability to his throne and length of days, in no way suffer oppression to approach the people intrusted to his care. For my own part I can with truth assert, that I have never so far lent myself to the indulgence of the world's pleasures as to forget that, however sweet to the appetite, they are more bitter in the issue than the most deadly poisons. Alas! for the jewels of this world which have been poured in such profusion upon my head: they bear no longer any value in my sight, neither do I any longer feel the slightest inclination to possess them. Have I ever contemplated with delight the graces of youth and beauty? The gratification is extinguished, it no longer exists in my nature. The enjoyments of hunting, and of social mirth, have too frequently been the source of pain and regret. The finger of old age has been held out to indicate that retirement must be my greatest solace, my surest resource, and from thence must be derived my highest advantages. In short, there neither is nor can be in this world any permanent state of repose or happiness; all is fleeting, vain, and perishable. In the twinkling of

an

an eye shall we see the enchantress which enslaves the world and its votaries, seize the throat of another and another victim; and so exposed is man to be trodden down by the calamities of life, that one might be almost persuaded to affirm that he never had existence. "That world, the end of which is destined to be thus miserable, can scarcely be worth the risk of so much useless violence."

If indeed, in contemplation of future contingencies, I have been sometimes led to deal with thieves and robbers with indiscriminate severity, whether during my minority or since my accession to the throne, never have I been actuated by motives of private interest or general ambition. The treachery and inconstancy of the world are to me as clear as the light of day. Of all that could be thought necessary to the enjoyment of life I have been singularly fortunate in the possession. In gold, and jewels, and sumptuous wardrobes, and in the choicest beauties the sun ever shone upon, what man has ever surpassed me? And had I then conducted myself without the strictest regard to the honour and happiness of God's creatures consigned to my care, I should have been the basest of oppressors.

But to descend to matters of less serious importance. At the period of which I am about to speak there were to be found in the province of Bengal performers in slight of hand, or jugglers,* of such unrivalled skill in their art, that I have thought a few instances of their extraordinary dexterity not unworthy of a place in these memorials. On one occasion in particular, there came to my court *seven* of these men, who confidently boasted that they were capable of producing effects so strange as far to surpass the scope of the human understanding: and most certainly when they proceeded to their operations, they exhibited in their performances things of so extraordinary a nature, as without the actual demonstration the world would not have conceived possible; such indeed as cannot but be considered among the most surprising circumstances of the age in which we live.

First. They stated that of any tree that should be named they would set the seed in the earth, and that I should immediately witness the extraordinary result. Khaun-e-Jahaun, one of the nobles present, observed that if they spoke truly, he should wish them to produce for his conviction a mulberry tree. The men arose without hesitation, and having in ten separate spots set some seed in the ground, they recited among themselves, in cabalistical language unintelligible to the standers-by, when instantly a plant was seen springing from each of the ten places, and each proved the tree required by Khaun-e-Jahaun. In the same manner they produced a mango, an apple tree, a cypress, a pine-apple, a fig tree, an

* Bauzigurs.

an almond, a walnut, and many more trees, and this without any attempt at concealment in the operation; but open to the observation of all present, the trees were perceived gradually and slowly springing from the earth, to the height of one, or perhaps of two cubits, when they shot forth leaves and branches; the apple tree in particular producing fruit, which fruit was brought to me, and I can attest to its fragrance.

The fact was not however confined to the apple tree alone, for having made the other trees appear in the manner above described, they said that if I thought fit to order it, I should taste of the fruit of every tree, which did not fail to increase the astonishment already excited. Then making a sort of procession round the trees as they stood, and invoking certain names, in a moment there appeared on the respective trees a sweet mango without the *rind*, an almond fresh and ripe, a large fig of the most delicious kind, and so with the pine, and every other tree of which they had set the seed, the fruit being pulled in my presence and brought to me, and every one present was allowed to taste of it. This, however, was not all; before the trees were removed there appeared among the foliage birds of such surprising beauty, in colour, and shape, and melody of song, as the world never saw before; and the more to confirm us in the reality, the birds were observed to whisper to each other, and to flutter, and contend with each other in playful indifference among the branches. At the close of the operation the foliage, as in autumn, was seen to put on its variegated tints, and the trees gradually disappeared into the earth from which they had been made to spring. I can only further observe, that if the circumstances which I have now described had not happened in my own presence, I could never have believed that they had any existence in reality.*

Secondly. One night, and in the very middle of the night, when half this globe was wrapped in darkness, one of these seven men stripped himself almost naked, and having spun himself swiftly round several times, he took a sheet with which he covered himself, and from beneath the sheet drew out a resplendent mirror, by the radiance of which a light so powerful was produced, as to have illuminated the hemisphere to an incredible distance round; to such a distance indeed, that we have the attestation of travellers to the fact, who declared that on a particular night, the same night on which the exhibition took place, and at the distance of ten days' journey, they saw the atmosphere so powerfully illuminated, as to exceed the brightness of the brightest day that they had ever seen. This also may be considered, I think, among the extraordinary things of the age.

O Thirdly.

* I have myself been witness to the mango operation, on the western side of India, but a sheet was employed to cover the process. I have, however, no conception of the means by which it was accomplished, unless the jugglers had the trees about them, in every stage, from the seedling to the fruit.

Thirdly. The seven men stood close together in a group, and without moving either lips or tongue, produced between them such harmony and sweetness of modulation, as if the whole seven had but one voice, and that forming the most delightful unison. It was at the same time distinctly ascertained that the mouth and tongue had not the slightest share in the operation.* This also afforded subject of admiration.

Fourthly. They made for themselves about an hundred air-bolts † (*teir-e-hawah*), which they placed on an elevated spot at two bow-shot distance from the spot on which they stood, informing me that they would cause any one, or as many of them as I chose to order, to explode or take fire, without stirring from their place, in my presence. This they accordingly did, and I do not question that they would have set fire to ten at once if I had thought fit.

Fifth. They placed in my presence a large seething-pot or cauldron, and filling it partly with water, they threw into it eight of the smaller maunns of Irâk of rice; when without the application of the smallest spark of fire the cauldron forthwith began to boil; in a little time they took off the lid, and drew from it near a hundred platters full,‡ each with a stewed fowl at top. This also may be considered among things extraordinary.

Sixth. On a dry spot of ground they placed a particular flower, and having danced round it three times successively, an ebullition of water shot up from the flower, and instantly a shower of roses fell on all below, while not a drop of moisture touched the ground. When this miraculous fountain had continued to play for more than an hour they removed the rose, or whatever else it might have been, and not a vestige of any thing humid appeared on the spot where it had been placed. Again: they placed the same flower on the ground, and it threw up at this time, alternately, water and flower-shedding fire, and this for nearly two parts of a watch of the day.

Seventh. One of the seven men stood upright before us, a second passed upwards along his body, and head to head, placed his feet upwards in the air. A third managed to climb up in the same manner, and planting his feet to those of the second, stood with his head upwards, and so alternately to the seventh, who crowned this extraordinary human pillar with his head uppermost; and what excited an extraordinary clamour of surprise, was to observe the first man, who thus supported on the crown of his head the whole of the other six, lift one foot as high as the shoulder, standing thus upon one leg, and exhibiting a degree of strength and steadiness not exactly within the scope of my comprehension.

Eighth. One of the men stood upright as before; another took hold of him by

* This doubtless was the effect of ventriloquism.

† Query, rockets or squibs.

‡ Lungry, or perhaps pungry.

by the hips from behind, and so on to the number of forty men, each laying hold the one of the other by the hips in the same manner. The first man put forth his strength, and contrived to force the whole of the others in train along the field for some time: a degree of bodily strength which could not be witnessed without considerable astonishment.

Ninth. They produced a man whom they divided limb from limb, actually severing his head from the body. They scattered these mutilated members along the ground, and in this state they lay for some time. They then extended a sheet or curtain over the spot, and one of the men putting himself under the sheet, in a few minutes came from below, followed by the individual supposed to have been cut into joints, in perfect health and condition, and one might have safely sworn that he had never received wound or injury whatever.

Tenth. They took a small bag, and having first shewn that it was entirely empty, one of them put his hand into the bag; on withdrawing his hand again, out came two game cocks of the largest size and great beauty, which immediately assailing each other, fought with such force and fury, that their wings emitted sparks of fire at every stroke. This continued for the full space of an astronomical hour, when they put an end to the combat by throwing a sheet over the animals. Again they withdrew the sheet, and there appeared a brace of partridges with the most beautiful and brilliant plumage, which immediately began to tune their throats as if there were nothing human present; pecking at worms with the same sort of chuckle (*kakkah*) as they are heard to use on the hill side. The sheet was now thrown, as in the other instance, over the partridges, and when again withdrawn, instead of those beautiful birds there appeared two frightful black snakes, with flat heads and crimson bellies, which, with open mouth and head erect, and coiled together, attacked each other with the greatest fury, and so continued to do, until, as it appeared, they became quite exhausted, when they fell asunder. The sheet was thrown over as before, and when finally withdrawn, there appeared not a vestige of the snakes or of any thing else.

Eleventh. They made an excavation in the earth in the shape of a tank or reservoir, of considerable dimensions, which they requested us to fill with water. When this was done they spread a covering over the place, and after a short interval having removed the cover, the water appeared to be one complete sheet of ice, and they desired that some of the elephant keepers might be directed to lead their elephants across. Accordingly one of the men set his elephant upon the ice, and the animal walked over with as much ease and safety as if it were a platform of solid rock, remaining for some time on the surface of the frozen pond without occasioning the slightest fracture in the ice. As usual, the sheet

was

was drawn across the place, and being again removed, every vestige of ice, and even moisture of any sort, had completely disappeared.

Twelfth. They caused two tents to be set up at the distance of a bow-shot the one from the other, the doors or entrances being placed exactly opposite; they raised the tent walls all around, and desired that it might be particularly observed that they were entirely empty. Then fixing the tent walls to the ground, two of the seven men entered, one into each tent, none other of the seven entering either of the tents. Thus prepared, they said they would undertake to bring out of the tents any animal we chose to mention, whether bird or beast, and set them in conflict with each other. Khaun-e-Jahaun, with a smile of incredulity, required them to shew us a battle between two ostriches. In a few minutes two ostriches of the largest size issued, one from either tent, and attacked each other with such fury that the blood was seen streaming from their heads; they were at the same time so equally matched, that neither could get the better of the other, and they were therefore separated by the men, and conveyed within the tents. My son Khoorum then called for the neilahgâo, and immediately were seen to issue from the tents two of those untameable animals, equally large, fat, and fierce, which likewise commenced a furious combat, seizing each other by the neck, and alternately forcing one another backwards and forwards for the space of nearly two guhrries of time, after which they were also separated, and withdrawn into the tents. In short, they continued to produce from either tent whatever animal we chose to name, and before our eyes set them to fight in the manner I have attempted to describe; and although I have exerted my utmost invention to discover the secret of the contrivance, it has hitherto been entirely without success.

Thirteenth. They were furnished with a bow and about fifty steel-pointed arrows. One of the seven men took the bow in hand, and shooting an arrow into the air, the shaft stood fixed at a considerable height; he shot a second arrow, which flew straight to the first, to which it became attached, and so with every one of the remaining arrows to the last of all, which striking the united sheaf suspended in the air, the whole immediately broke asunder, and came at once to the earth. This also it would be difficult to explain.

Fourteenth. They filled a large vessel full of water perfectly transparent, and placed it on the floor before me. One of them held in his hand a red rose, which he said, by giving it a dip into the water, he would bring out of any colour I chose to mention. Accordingly he gave the rose a plunge, and out it came of a bright yellow; and thus at every dip he brought it out of a different kind and colour; at one time a gûlaul, at another an orange blossom. In short, a hundred times repeated he would have produced at each a flower of a different

different kind and colour. They then plunged a skein of white thread into the vessel, and brought it first of a red, then of a yellow colour, and so of a different colour a hundred times repeated, if required so to do.

Fifteenth. They produced a bird-cage, of which the side that appeared next to me exhibited a pair of sweet-singing nightingales. They gave the cage a turn, and though there was no partition to divide it, there now appeared a couple of beautiful green parrots. Another turn of the cage, and they shewed us another sort of speaking bird of a scarlet colour: another, and we saw a brace of partridges beautifully mottled and coloured, and, what appears extraordinary, of most melodious song. Thus at every change of the four sides of the cage, there appeared a different kind of bird at every change, and the like if repeated a hundred times. This must, I think, have been attended with the greatest difficulty in the performance.

Sixteenth. They spread out a carpet of twenty cubits in length, and of very beautiful colours and pattern. They turned it upside downwards, and displayed a pattern and colours entirely different; and in like manner at every turn, if an hundred times repeated, the carpet would exhibit patterns and colours entirely different, *ad infinitum*.

Seventeenth. They brought a large ewer, which in my presence they filled full of water. They reversed the ewer with its face downwards, spilling the water to the last drop: they turned the vessel with its face upwards, and it appeared as full of water as at first. And this they could have repeated an hundred times over with the same effect; which I could not but consider equally curious and unaccountable.

Eighteenth. They produced a large sack, open at both ends. At one end of this they introduced a melon, which at the other end was brought out a cucumber. Then the cucumber at one end came out at the other a noble bunch the finest grapes. Again, they introduced the grapes at one end, and at the other out came a bag of apples, of the true abbas sort: and thus, in an hundred instances, if required, they would in each instance exhibit a similar change: all which could not but appear extraordinary to the eye.

Nineteenth. One of the seven men stood up before me, and setting open his mouth, immediately out came the head of a snake. Another of the men seized the snake by the neck, and drew it out to the length of four cubits. This being disposed of by casting it to the ground, another followed in the same manner, and so on to the number of eight, none of them less than four or five cubits in length. These being all cast loose upon the ground, were immediately seen writhing in the folds of each other, and tearing one another with the greatest apparent fury: a spectacle not less strange than frightful.

Twentieth. They took a looking-glass in one hand, and in the other a rose, or other

other flower of any colour at will. They held the flower for an instant behind the mirror, and bringing it forward again, it had assumed a different colour. Thus it became alternately changed by this sort of sleight, to green, and red, and orange, and violet, and black and white: very curious to behold.

Twenty-first. They arranged in my presence ten empty porcelain jars, all in attendance having witnessed that they were actually and entirely empty. In about half an hour they uncovered the jars, when, to our surprise, one was found to be full of wheat, another of preserves, another of sugar-candy, another of different sorts of pickles, another of ladies'-legs,* another of citron, and another of tamarind. In short, every one of the jars contained a different eatable of some kind or other, which was presented to me, and tasted by most of those who were in attendance. After a little space they uncovered the jars for the last time, and they were seen to be completely empty, and as clean as if they had been an hundred times washed in the purest spring water. This also was considered something strange and surprising.

Twenty-second. They brought the Koulliaut-e-Saady, or works of Saady, and in my presence deposited it in a small bag, of course previously examined. They drew out the book, and it had been transformed into the Diwaun of Hafez; and the latter being replaced in the bag, it was drawn out again as the Diwaun of Sûliman. This was repeated many times, and every time a work was drawn out different from that which was last returned into the bag.

Twenty-third. They produced a chain of fifty cubits in length, and in my presence threw one end of it towards the sky, where it remained as if fastened to something in the air. A dog was then brought forward, and being placed at the lower end of the chain, immediately ran up, and reaching the other end, immediately disappeared in the air. In the same manner a hog, a panther, a lion, and a tiger, were alternately sent up the chain, and all equally disappeared at the upper end of the chain. At last they took down the chain and put it into a bag, no one even discovering in what way the different animals were made to vanish into the air in the mysterious manner above described. This, I may venture to affirm, was beyond measure strange and surprising.

Twenty-fourth. They placed before me a large covered basket,† having first shewn to my satisfaction that it was quite empty. Having claimed my attention, they now took up the cover, and the basket appeared brimful of the choicest viands, most delicious to the taste. They put on the cover, and again in a few minutes lifting it up, the basket now appeared full of fellouny,‡ raisins, almonds, and

* I have no idea what this refers to. We certainly have a pear to which is sometimes given the name of *Cuisse Madame*.

† Lungry: if not a basket, I know not whatit was.

‡ What this is I cannot tell, unless it refers to the following article, raisins; in which case it might be Cephalonia raisins.

and other dried fruits and aromatic herbs. [The third remove is indicated in a hand-writing so totally unintelligible in the Persian copy, that I have not attempted to render it.] In short, at every alternate removal of the basket-lid, though an hundred times repeated, a fresh display of delicacies would be presented to the spectator, to our great admiration and surprise.

Twenty-fifth. They caused to be set before me a large covered basin, which they filled with water. They took off the cover to shew that it contained nothing but water; it was now replaced, but being again removed, there appeared in the water ten or a dozen green leaves. The basket was again closed, and, on being re-opened, there appeared three or four large snakes coiled together in the water. Another covering and removal, and there appeared in the water five or six koully khaur.* At the last uncovering of the vessel it was found to contain neither water nor any thing else, but was entirely empty.

Twenty-sixth. One of the men in my presence displayed on his little finger a ruby ring; he removed the ring to another finger, and the gem had taken the colour of an emerald; removed to another finger, and the emerald became a diamond; again removed, and the diamond became a turquoise: and this repeated for any number of times, terminated in the same result, every change producing a gem of a different colour and kind.

Twenty-seventh. A two-edged sword was set up, with the hilt strongly fastened in the earth, and one of the men brought his naked side to bear upon it in such a manner, as to excite the utmost surprise that he should have received no bodily injury from having brought himself into such contact with so keen a weapon. [This passage is so extremely ill written in the Persian copy, that it has been hardly possible to obtain the precise meaning.]

Twenty-eighth. They produced a blank volume of the purest white paper, which was placed in my hands, to shew that it contained neither figures nor coloured pages whatever, of which I satisfied myself and all around. One of the men took the volume in hand, and the first opening exhibited a page of bright red sprinkled with gold, forming a blank tablet splendidly elaborate. The next turn presented a leaf of beautiful azure, sprinkled in the same manner, and exhibiting on the margins numbers of men and women in various attitudes. The juggler then turned to another leaf, which appeared of a Chinese colour and fabric, and sprinkled in the same manner with gold; but on it were delineated herds of cattle and lions, the latter seizing upon the kine in a manner that I never observed in any other paintings. The next leaf exhibited was of a beautiful green, similarly powdered with gold, on which was represented in lively colours a garden, with numerous cypresses, roses,

* Possibly cranes, or some large bird of the kind.

roses, and other flowering shrubs in full bloom, and in the midst of the garden an elegant pavilion. The next change exhibited a leaf of orange in the same manner powdered with gold, on which the painter had delineated the representation of a great battle, in which two adverse kings were seen engaged in the struggles of a mortal conflict. In short, at every turn of the leaf a different colour, scene, and action, was exhibited, such as was indeed most pleasing to behold. But of all the performances, this latter of the volume of paper, was that which afforded me the greatest delight, so many beautiful pictures and extraordinary changes having been brought under view, that I must confess my utter inability to do justice in the description. I can only add, that although I had frequently in my father's court witnessed such performances, never did I see or hear of any thing in execution so wonderfully strange, as was exhibited with apparent facility by these seven jugglers. I dismissed them finally with a donation of fifty thousand rupees, with the intimation that all the ameirs of my court, from the order of one thousand upwards, should each contribute something in proportion.

In very truth, however we may have bestowed upon these performances the character of trick or juggle, they very evidently partake of the nature of something beyond the exertion of human energy; at all events, such performances were executed with inimitable skill, and if there were in the execution any thing of facility, what should prevent their accomplishment by any man of ordinary capacity? I have heard it stated that the art has been called the Semnanian (perhaps *asmaunian*, 'celestial'), and I am informed that it is also known and practised to a considerable extent among the nations of Europe. It may be said, indeed, that there exists in some men a peculiar and essential faculty which enables them to accomplish things far beyond the ordinary scope of human exertion, such as frequently to baffle the utmost subtilty of the understanding to penetrate.*

I shall here take upon me to relate, that once upon a time a native of Arabia, who had passed the age of forty, was brought to the metropolis for the purpose of being presented to me. When introduced to my presence, I observed that he had lost his arm close to the shoulder, and it occurred to me to ask him whether this was his condition from his birth, or whether it was an injury which he had received in battle. He seemed considerably embarrassed by the question; but stated that the accident which had deprived him of his arm was attended with circumstances so very extraordinary, as to be rather beyond credibility, and might perhaps expose him to some degree of ridicule: he had therefore made a vow never to describe it. On my importuning him further, however, and urging that

* The latter part of this passage is one among the many that, through the unaccountable ignorance of the person who copied the Persian memoir, I have found no small difficulty in rendering into common sense.

that there could exist no reason for concealment compatible with what he owed me for my protection, he finally relented, and related what follows.

"When I was about the age of fifteen, it happened to me to accompany my father on a voyage to India; and at the expiration of about sixty days, during which we had wandered in different directions through the ocean, we were assailed by a storm so dreadful, as to be for ever impressed upon my recollection. For three days and three nights successively it raged with such indescribable fury, the sea rose in such tremendous surges, the rain descended in such torrents, and the peals of thunder accompanied by lightning so incessant, as to be terrific in the utmost degree. To complete the horrors of our situation, the ship's mast, which was as large in compass as two men with arms extended could encircle, snapped in the middle, and falling upon the deck, destroyed many of the crew. The vessel was therefore on the very verge of foundering; but the tempest subsiding at the close of the third day, we were for the present preserved from destruction, although we were driven far from the course which led to the port of our destination.

"When, however, the ship had for some days been pursuing this uncertain course, we came in sight unexpectedly of what appeared to be a lofty mountain in the midst of the ocean; and as we neared the spot it was soon ascertained to be an island, covered with numerous buildings, and interspersed with trees and river streams in most agreeable variety. Our stock of water in the ship was nearly exhausted, and we therefore steered close in land; and from certain fishermen who were out in their boats we now learnt that the island was in possession of the Portuguese Franks; that it was extremely populous, and that there were no Mussulmen inhabitants; moreover, that they had no intercourse with strangers.

"To be as brief as possible: as soon as the ship had reached the anchoring ground and dropped her anchor, a Portuguese captain and another officer came on board; and instantly, without leaving even an infant child to take care of the ship, conveyed the whole of the ship's company, passengers and all, in boats to the shore; desiring, at the same time, that we might not be under any apprehensions, for that as soon as it could be discovered that there was among us a person that suited a particular purpose, which they did not chuse to explain, that one alone would be detained, and the others dismissed without injury. The port being theirs, and ourselves entirely at their mercy, we were compelled to submit to all they said; and accordingly the whole ship's company, merchants, slaves, and mariners, to the number of twelve hundred persons, were all crowded into one house.

"From thence they sent for us one by one alternately, and stripping us stark-

 naked,

naked, one of their hakeims, or physicians, proceeded to make the minutest examination of our bodies, in every muscle, vein, and limb, telling each respectively after undergoing such examination, that he was at liberty to go about his business. This they continued to do until it came to the turn of myself and a brother who was with us; and what was our dismay and horror when, after the described examination, the hakeim delivered us into the custody of some of the people in attendance, with orders to place us behind the curtain; that is, where we should not be open to human intercourse. With the exception of my brother and myself, the whole of the ship's company, on whose bodies they failed to discover the marks of which they were in search, were now dismissed. Neither could my father either by tears or remonstrances succeed in diverting them from their purpose; to his repeated demands to know in what his sons could have offended, that out of a ship's company of twelve hundred persons they alone should be detained, they replied only by a frown, utterly disregarding every intreaty.

"They now conveyed my brother and myself to a part of the place where they lodged us in separate chambers, opposite however to each other. Every morning they brought us for food fowl kabaubs, honey, and white bread, and this continued for the space of ten days. At the expiration of that period the naokhoda (or commander of the ship), demanded permission to proceed on his voyage. My father implored that he would delay his departure, if it were only for two or three days longer, when peradventure the Portuguese might be induced to give up his sons. He presented himself to the ruler of the port, and again by the most humble intreaties endeavoured to obtain our release, but in vain.

"The same medical person on whose report we were detained now came with ten other Franks to the house or chamber where my brother was confined, and again stripping him naked, they laid him on his back on a board or table, where he was exposed to the same manual examination as before. They then left him and came to me, and stretching me out on a board in the same manner and plight, again examined my body in every part as before. Again they returned to my brother; for from the situation of our prisons, the doors being exactly opposite, I could distinctly observe all that passed. They sent for a large bowl and a knife, and placing my brocher with his head over the bowl, and his cries and supplications all in vain, they struck him over the mouth, and with the knife actually severed his head from the body, both the head and his blood being received in the bowl. When the bleeding had ceased they took away the bowl of blood, which they immediately poured into a pot of boiling oil brought for the purpose, stirring the whole together with a ladle until both blood and oil

oil became completely amalgamated. Will it be believed, that after this they took the head and again fixing it exactly to the body, they continued to rub the adjoining parts with the mixture of blood and oil until the whole had been applied. They left my brother in this state, closed the door, and went their way.

"At the expiration of three days from this, they sent for me from my place of confinement, and telling me that they had obtained at my brother's expense all that was necessary to their purpose, they pointed out to me the entrance to a place under ground, which they said was the repository of gold and jewels to an incalculable amount. Thither they informed me I was to descend, and that I might bring away for myself as much of the contents as I had strength to carry. At first I refused all belief to their assertions, conceiving that doubtless they were about to send me where I was to be exposed to some tremendous trial; but as their importunities were too well enforced, I had no alternative but submission.

"I entered the opening which led to the passage, and having descended a flight of stairs about fifty steps, I discovered four separate chambers. In the first chamber, to my utter surprise, I beheld my brother apparently restored to perfect health. He wore the dress and habiliments of the Ferenguies, or Portuguese, had on his head a cap of the same people, profusely ornamented with pearl and precious stones, a sword set with diamonds by his side, and a staff similarly enriched under his arm. My surprise was not diminished when the moment he observed me I saw him turn away from me, as if under feelings of the utmost disgust and disdain. I became so alarmed at a reception so strange and unaccountable, that although I saw that it was my own brother, the very marrow in my bones seemed to have been turned into cold water. I ventured, however, to look into the second chamber, and there I beheld heaps upon heaps of diamonds and rubies, and pearl and emeralds, and every other description of precious stones, thrown one on the other in astonishing profusion. The third chamber into which I looked contained in similar heaps an immense profusion of gold; and the fourth chamber was strewed middle deep with silver.

"I had some difficulty in determining to which of these glittering deposits I should give the preference. At last I recollected that a single diamond was of greater value than all the gold I could gather into my robe, and I accordingly decided on tucking up my skirts and filling them with jewels. I put out my hand in order to take up some of these glittering articles, when from some invisible agent, perhaps it was the effect of some overpowering effluvia, I received a blow so stunning, that I found it impossible to stand in the place any longer. In my retreat, it was necessary to pass the chamber in which I had seen my brother.

The instant he perceived me about to pass he drew his sword, and made a furious cut at me. I endeavoured to avoid the stroke by suddenly starting aside, but in vain; the blow took effect, and my right arm dropped from the shoulder-joint. Thus wounded and bleeding, I rushed from this deposit of treasure and horror, and at the entrance above found the physician and his associates, who had so mysteriously determined the destiny of my unhappy brother. Some of them went below and brought away my mutilated arm; and having closed up the entrance with stone and mortar, conducted me, together with my arm all bleeding as I was, to the presence of the Portuguese governor, men and women, and children, flocking to the doors to behold the extraordinary spectacle.

"The wound in my shoulder continued to bleed; but having received from the governor a compensation of three thousand tomauns, a horse with jewelled caparison, a number of beautiful female slaves, and many males, with the promise of future favour in reserve, the Portuguese physician was ordered to send for me, and applying some styptic preparation to the wound it quickly healed, and so perfectly, that it might be said I was thus armless from my birth. I was then dismissed, and having shortly afterwards obtained a passage in another ship, in about a month from my departure reached the port for which I was destined."*

On the above relation, continues our imperial memorialist, I have to observe, that in all probability the extraordinary circumstances to which it refers were effected through the operations of chimia ('alchemy'), known to be extensively practised among the Franks, and in which the jugglers from Bengal appear to have been very well instructed.

Another marvellous relation which I am led to introduce into my narrative, is that which refers to the origin of the stupendous fortress of Mandou, one of the most celebrated in Hindûstaun, and which we are taught to believe derived its existence from the following circumstances.

A poor inhabitant of one of the cities in Hindûstaun, by repairing with his axe to one of the neighbouring woody hills every day, and bringing to town at night such fuel as he was able to collect, contrived with the produce to provide the scanty means of subsistence for his family. Occasionally, as necessity required it, he was in the habit of taking his axe to a smith for the purpose of getting the edge restored: but on one occasion his hatchet glancing aside from a billet of wood struck a stone, which stone happened to be that which possesses the quality of changing iron into gold: the effect was that the woodman's hatchet was immediately transmuted into a wedge of gold. In the extreme of ignorance and folly

* The story of the Arab would make a respectable addition to the voyages of Sinbad in the Arabian Nights.

folly the woodman again took his hatchet to the smith. "This is a pretty sort of job," said he, "that you have done by my hatchet, the edge is not only destroyed but the instrument by which I earned my bread is turned into copper." The smith, being much better informed than his customer, told him that certainly his hatchet was now not worth repairing, and that if he chose, as it was but just that he should make good the injury, he would give him a new one in its stead. But come," said he, "Shew us the stone which has spoilt your hatchet by turning it into copper." The silly rustic took him to the spot without hesitation, and pointed out the stone, which, with a joy not difficult to imagine the wary smith instantly conveyed home, where without divulging the secret of his precious deposit to wife or child or any one else, he locked it up most carefully in his chest. He did not, however, dismiss the poor wood-cutter without giving him an excellent new hatchet according to promise.

The fortunate blacksmith now proceeded by degrees to turn every bit of iron in his possession into gold. In process of time he built for himself a sumptuous palace. He entertained in his service numbers of armed men, all clad in coats of mail, and all experienced in the trade of war, to many or most of whom he assigned yearly stipends of from two to three hundred tomauns * a man. In short, the fame of his bounty and liberal encouragement to those who enrolled themselves under his standard extended to all parts of the world, and men of talent and courage from every region flocked to his presence, and were sure of a kind and generous reception.

This, as may well be imagined, could make but little impression on a treasury, which derived its means from a source so inexhaustible. He became however anxious to secure for himself and treasures some place of strength, to resist any attempt of superior power which on any future occasion might be disposed to assail him. He accordingly selected for his purpose four lofty contiguous hills, which, lifting their summits to the skies, contained within their precincts a spacious and extensive plain; and these he determined to fortify by all the means to be derived from the art of war and the science of defence.

In short he commenced his operations without further delay, by setting twenty thousand masons and pioneers, under his own directions, to carry on the works on one side of the position which he had fixed upon, while his son with an equal number of workmen was similarly employed on the opposite side; until at the termination of thirty years,† father and son met together, and the two extremities of the stupendous work became thus united. The fortifications thus completed

* From 6,600 to 9,900 rupees.

† This should probably be three, as thirty years would be rather too large a proportion of the smith's life.

pleted, extended to little less than fourteen farsangs in circumference;* and as to the expense incurred in the execution of such an undertaking, it would surpass the power of words or writing to form an estimate.

In order to facilitate the communications with the exterior, the fortress contained ten large gateways and four sally-ports in different directions; and from each of the gateways, which were erected on lofty eminences,† a flight of steps cut in the solid rock led from top to bottom of the mountain, making altogether fifty thousand steps; that is, properly speaking, a staircase of five thousand steps to every principal gateway. He built, moreover, within the fortifications a lofty and spacious mosque, containing one thousand chambers, or perhaps cloisters, each chamber or *seffah* containing a pulpit for the recitation of the khotbah and other services of religion on Fridays; and such in a short time was the multitude of human beings accumulated within the circuit of this stupendous fortress, that on occasions of public worship the whole of the thousand and one oratories were completely crowded. Parallel with the mosque, or contiguous to it, he built also an extensive karavanserâi, and a lofty dome or rotunda; this latter to serve as the burial-place of his family. In this dome it is moreover described that they introduced four warm-water springs, the contents of which being made to drop slowly, drop by drop, gradually formed a petrified mass of such solidity and magnitude, as to supply for his children, and others bound to him by the ties of affection, a material for their tombs, superior to, and more delicate than the finest marble.

To bring the matter within as short a compass as possible, when this sumptuous place of worship and its appurtenances had been completed, and the country round for the space of a month's journey in circuit had been subjugated to the authority of our fortunate blacksmith, an ambassador from the monarch of Bûrhanpour arrived at Mandou, to solicit the hand of his daughter for the son of that monarch, the prince of Bûrhanpour. Having signified his assent to this arrangement, he took some time to prepare the suitable equipments, and the requisite paraphernalia for the bride: after which she was formally delivered to the ambassador to be conducted to Bûrhanpour. On the departure of his daughter, however, the royal blacksmith deposited in her palanquin, and sealed up in a purse of cloth of gold, this inestimable gold-creating stone: and she was instructed to acquaint the monarch that on parting with her, her father should have said that for a single methkal, or scruple of that stone, worthless as it seemed,

* The fortifications of Mandou were doubtless of great extent; but probably fourteen kôsse would be nearer the truth than fourteen farsangs: twenty-one, instead of forty-two miles.

† For greater convenience and cover, the gateways would be better placed in the hollows between the hills. The towers usually erected to defend the gateway have however a lofty appearance.

seemed, he would not have taken a thousand tomauns of gold; nevertheless, from the excess of his affection to his child, he had resigned to her this inestimable jewel. At the same time he explained to her the miraculous properties of the stone; conceiving that from his simple statement alone of its extraordinary value, without further particulars, the monarch of Bûrhanpour would be led to conclude that there was something very wonderful connected with this stone, and that it must contain some very mysterious latent property.

Under the care of the ambassador, who was also hâjeb, or lord chamberlain of his court, the princess of Mandou, accompanied by a suitable retinue of her father's people, set off for Bûrhanpour, the well known city of that name on the river Tapty, and having proceeded to a river, (without doubt the Nerbuddah), within four days journey from that city, she was there met by the Bûrhanpourian with a numerous escort of his nobles, an imperial and sumptuous suit of tents having been set up for her reception on the banks of the river. Having bestowed upon the princess and her retinue the usual marks of royal bounty, in khelaats, and gold, and beautiful horses, and in other respects liberally discharged the duties of hospitality, he was a little disappointed when, viewing her equipment, he could discover nothing that bespoke the splendour of a royal bride; and he could not forbear observing that as her father did not appear to have sent with her immediately any part of her marriage portion, peradventure it was his intention to supply this defect at a future opportunity.

The daughter of the royal blacksmith now thought fit to apprize the monarch of Bûrhanpour, that on taking leave, her father had presented her with a bag of gold brocade containing a jewel, the weight of a methkal of which was equal in value to the revenue of a hundred provinces: at the same time she had been instructed, when inquiry should be made as to the jewels and other appendages of royal splendour which were expected to accompany her, to present to the Bûrhanpourian monarch that same bag of brocade; with which, the princess laid the bag on the floor, before her intended father-in-law. The prince of Bûrhanpour on disclosing the bag, and perceiving nought but the stone, which in appearance exhibited nothing very remarkable, expressed considerable displeasure; and suspecting that the *brocaded purse* with its *stone contents* had been transmitted with no other view than to indicate the opinion entertained of his character, he indignantly snatched the stone from the hands of the princess, and threw it into the middle of the river. From the same spot, without further ceremony, he dismissed the princess and sent her back to Mandou to the presence of her father.

The chief of Mandou, on the return of his daughter thus dishonoured, took no further notice of the insult than by transmitting a letter to the Bûrhanpourian

conceived

conceived in the following terms: "The article which I sent thee by my daughter, and of which thou hadst not the common sense to understand the value, would have produced thee every day gold by the horse-load. Hast thou had the folly to cast it into the Nerbuddah, from whence it can never more be recovered?" It is needless to expatiate upon the regret and remorse of the king of Bûrhanpour, when on receipt of this epistle he came to understand the extent of his error: and although he employed every exertion and expedient to search the bed of the river, not a vestige of this most precious of stones was ever found.

Ages afterwards, when my father Akbar set on foot his expedition against a subsequent monarch of Bûrhanpour, one of the elephants in the imperial train from its furious and intractable temper had a ponderous iron chain* attached to one of its legs. In passing this same river, the Nerbuddah, the chain came in contact with this long-lost and mysterious pebble, and when seen on the opposite side of the ford, was discovered to have been transmuted into solid gold.† The circumstance was immediately made known to my father, and a number of people was forthwith employed to search the ford, in the hope that something might be discovered of this miraculous substance; but entirely without success, and the search was of course abandoned in despair.

Of this celebrated fortress of Mandóu it remains to add, that notwithstanding every advantage of strength and situation, my father, after a siege of six months, made himself master of the place; when he caused the gateways, towers, and ramparts, together with the city within, to be entirely dismantled and laid in ruins, for the possession of this formidable strong-hold had but too frequently led its possessors into rebellion against their sovereign. The dependencies, lands, and inhabitants of the province, continued however as flourishing, if not more so, than ever, notwithstanding the destruction of Mandou.

I have yet further to observe, that at the period when I found it necessary to erect my victorious standard for the purpose of chastising the refractory rulers of the south of India, I came to the vicinity of this celebrated place, and ascended to view its stupendous ruins. I found the walls only demolished in part, and I became so highly delighted with the freshness and salubrity of the air and climate, that I determined to restore the town. For this purpose I accordingly ordered the foundation to be marked out, among the ruins of the ancient city, of a variety of spacious and lofty structures of every description, which were carried to a completion in a much shorter time than might have been expected. I continued

* Seven hundred mauns, at twenty-eight pounds to the maun, would be ten tons lacking four hundred-weight, which is incredible!

† It cannot be denied that the imperial biographer has here taxed the credulity of his readers to the utmost limits: ten tons of gold would make 1,260,000 guineas.

I continued to reside there for one whole year, during which I laid out, moreover, several fine gardens, with beautiful water-works and cascades; and the members of my court and camp, actively emulating the example of their sovereign, soon filled the place in every part with palaces and gardens, of similar beauty and description.

My favourite son Khoorum had concluded a treaty with Auddel Khaun and the princes of the Dekkan, by which it was agreed to put my lieutenants in possession of the best and most flourishing parts of the country, and among others of the city or town of Puttun,* celebrated for its manufacture of cloth of gold, such as is not to be met with elsewhere in all India. Often had my father declared, that whenever this place should come into his possession, he would build the walls with alternate wedges of gold and silver; and in very truth the place is not unworthy of such a cincture, however gorgeous and costly. Another of the towns ceded by the same treaty was Ahmednuggur, the metropolis of Husseyne Nizam Shah; and we shall add Khânapour, a district which for verdure of landscape and deliciousness of climate has not any where its equal. Another of the acquisitions derived from this treaty was the province of Berâr, of a month's journey in compass, and for its numerous towns and flourishing population equal to any part of Hindûstaun. All these were now transferred to my sovereign authority, together with a train of elephants four hundred in number, of the highest value for size and courage; these were furnished with caparisons, chains, neck-fastenings, and bells, all of gold, each of them bearing on its equipments not less than five maunns Hindy, equal to fifty maunns of Irâk of gold.† The velvet housings of the elephants had on them, moreover, the figures of various kinds of animals embroidered in pearl; and among the peishkesh, or presents of homage, conveyed to me on this occasion, were three chaplets of pearl, each chaplet moderately valued at sixty thousand rupees; and of every kind of precious stone, diamonds, rubies, and emeralds, and other articles of the most costly description, such a quantity was conveyed to my treasury and wardrobe as it would be unnecessarily tedious to enumerate.

At the intercession of Khoorum, after all, through whom their prayer was conveyed on the occasion, I gave up to the vanquished chiefs several districts or townships, as well for the maintenance of some degree of state, as from my royal disposition to forget the past, and as far as possible to heal the wounds

 of

* This is the celebrated Sidpoor Puttun, founded in the twelfth century by Sidraj Jey Sing, sovereign of Anhulwarra Puttun,—the Nehrwala of European geographers. They are about twenty miles apart, and both on the Sarasvati.

† At twenty-eight pounds to the maunn this would give one hundred and forty pounds weight of gold; which at sixty-three guineas to the pound, would make eight thousand eight hundred and twenty guineas four hundred times repeated!

of discomfiture. In fact, I restored great part of the territory subjugated by my armies in the field, reserving to myself only the honours of the coinage and khotbah, or invocation from the pulpits. At the same time I consigned the government of the conquered countries, with unlimited powers, to Khaun Khanan, whom I have long since learnt to regard as if he were mine own son or brother.

At the period when Sûltan Khoorum came to visit me from Bûrhanpour, he brought with him Oustaud Mahommed Nâë (the piper), whom he introduced to me as the most skilful musician of the age, adding moreover, that he had composed a particular melody which he had dignified with my name.* But beyond all, he was particularly celebrated for his unrivalled performance, as his name implied, upon the flageolet. In truth, when he proceeded to exhibit the prowess of his superior skill in my presence, he produced from his instruments such exquisite strains as absolutely burst upon the ear, so surprising were the effects of his performance. I experienced at all events such delight on the occasion, that I commanded a pair of scales to be brought before me, in order that I might reward him with his weight in gold. Without uttering a syllable the man abruptly quitted my presence; but immediately afterwards returning, he appeared with the piece of music fixed to one arm, and a little girl of about six years of age on the other; and he stated in explanation, that when he composed the melody this his little daughter was in his arms, and he therefore could not persuade himself that she was not entitled to share in my bounty. I nodded assent. He was placed in one of the scales and a quantity of gold in the other, and his weight was found to be five maunns Hindy. I ordered him to be weighed the second time, and the weight in gold to be given to the daughter.

Such, however, was the rapacious avarice and absence of all sense of propriety in this man, that in spite of the expostulations of the treasurers, he was not to be restrained from the most ludicrous attempts to increase the weight of gold; and his disrespect and want of decorum became so glaring that it was not to be overlooked, and I at last ordered him to be turned out of my camp. Before I proceeded to this extremity he had, however, had the assurance to demand that I should order him the daily supply of a camel-load of water, which further convinced me that there were no bounds to the man's insolence; and thus was the merit he possessed completely marred by the sordid spirit of avarice. Neither is it to be forgotten, that there are few defects among mankind of a more pernicious tendency than that want of sober respect, which is always due to those invested with the functions of sovereign authority. It subsequently appeared, however, that this was not the first time the man had been punished for

* Sout-e-Jahânguеiry.

for his folly, for Auddal Khaun had formerly driven him from his capital for a similar instance of insatiate avarice.

While my court continued at Mandou on this occasion, it came to my knowledge that Mirza Rûstum had, in some way or other, accumulated debts to the amount of four thousand tomauns, and his creditors were become extremely clamorous in their demands for payment, notwithstanding that he derived from his dignity of a commander of five thousand, an annual income of nearly thirty-two laks of rupees, independently of occasional presents, and other proofs of my bounty. This was a debt, however contracted, whether through extravagant habits or improvident management, from which there was no great probability that he would ever he able to relieve himself. As I could never discover that he was at any time devoted to singers, or that description of persons, I could not avoid suspecting that those whom he employed had taken a dishonest advantage of his indolence. Considering, therefore, that his energies would have been altogether extinguished under such a load of debt, I summoned the creditors to my presence, and immediately discharged the whole of it; at the same time desiring it to be understood, that, for the future, whoever gave credit to Mirza Rûstum, under any circumstances, would be subject to a penalty to the full amount of the debt, be it great or be it small.

As a considerable period had elapsed since I had an opportunity of visiting the province of Gûjerat, I felt a desire now I was in the neighbourhood to view it in its present state, and I accordingly quitted Mandou, after making the necessary preparations, and proceeded in that direction. When my father had completed the subjugation of the province, he had particularly enjoined every member of his court to erect at different stations on the frontiers convenient buildings, with gardens attached, and every requisite whether for repose or recreation. Now when we approached the capital of the province, the first place at which I encamped happened to be the villa and gardens of Khaun Khanan, close to the suburbs of Ahmedabad. Kheyr-ul-Nessa Begum, the daughter of that nobleman, who was present among the inmates of my harram, now came to me, and stating her wish to entertain me in these gardens of her father, requested that I would remain upon the spot for a few days, while she expedited the necessary arrangements for my reception. With a request which had its source in such motives of kindness I could not refuse to comply, and I accordingly continued encamped in the neighbourhood. I must not omit to observe by the way, that it was during that season of the year in which, from the effects of the cold weather, most trees and shrubs usually shedtheir foliage, and are equally bare of leaf, and fruit, and blossom.

 In

* About 605,000 rupees, at thirty-three to the tomaun.

In the course of five days, by employing various artificers of Ahmedabad, to the number of four hundred individuals, in different branches of decoration, she had so effectually changed the appearance of the gardens, by making use of coloured paper and wax, that every tree and shrub seemed as abundantly furnished with leaf, and flower, and fruit, as if in the very freshness and bloom of spring and summer. These included the orange, lemon, peach, pomegranate, and apple; and among flowering shrubs, of every species of rose, and other garden flowers of every description. So perfect, indeed, was the deception produced, that when I first entered the garden it entirely escaped my recollection that it was no longer the spring of the year, nor the season for fruit, and I unwittingly began to pluck at the fruit and flowers, the artificers having copied the beauties of nature with such surprising truth and accuracy. You might have said, without contradiction, that it was the very fruit and flower you saw, in all its bloom and freshness. The different avenues throughout the garden were at the same time furnished with a variety of tents and canopies, of velvet of the deepest green; so that these, together with the verdure of the sod, contrasted with the variegated and lively tints of the rose and an infinity of other flowers, left altogether such an impression on my mind, as that in the very season of the rose I never contemplated in any place, garden, or otherwise, any thing that afforded equal delight to the senses.

From this scene of fascination and enchantment I was not permitted to withdraw myself for three days and as many nights; during which, independently of the delicious repasts on which we feasted, the females of my harram by whom I was accompanied, to the number of four hundred, were each of them presented with a tray of four pieces of cloth of gold of the manufacture of Khorassaun, and an ambertchei, or perfume-stand, of elaborate workmanship and considerable value; none of which presents could have been estimated separately at a less sum than three hundred tomauns.* What the begum presented to myself on the occasion, in jewels, pieces of the richest fabric for my wardrobe, and horses of the highest value for temper and speed, could not have amounted to a less sum than four laks of rupees. In return, I presented her with a chaplet of pearl of the value of five laks of rupees, which had been purchased for my own use, and a bulse of rubies worth three laks more: I also added one thousand horse to the dignity already possessed by her father. In conclusion, what was thus exhibited in one short week, and in the very depth of winter, for my recreation, by the daughter of Khaun Khanan alone, could scarcely have been accomplished by the united genius and skill of any hundred individuals of the other sex, chuse them where you may.

When

* 9,900 rupees, which multiplied by 400 would make no inconsiderable sum.

When I at last entered the metropolis of Gûjerat on this occasion, I caused the buildings erected by my father for the greatest part, such at least as in my eyes appeared unworthy of his memory, to be demolished, and others of greater magnificence to be erected in their stead. I remained in the province for a period of five months, amusing myself in the sports of the field, and making excursions to view the different parts of the country. It is but justice to say, that its chief city, Ahmedabad, must be considered among the most renowned in Hindûstaun, when it is remembered, that during the time of the refractory Mirzas, who furnished so much employment to the armies of my father, an imperial nuggaurah, or noubet, sounded from five different quarters of the place, indicating the residence of as many independent sovereigns; and its magnitude may be further estimated by the fact, that it is surrounded by sixty-one suburbs, each separately as large as a moderate-sized town, and each governed by its own separate magistrate. There were moreover, at the time, in the different bazars of the city, not less than five thousand bankers' or money-changers' shops: from all which circumstances taken together, we might with a single glance of the eye, conclude as to the greatness and opulence of this very magnificent city.

In the midst of its numerous population it contains, however, an extraordinary proportion of thieves and vagabonds of every description, so inured to robberies and violence, as not to be deterred from their profligate habits of life by the severest measures that I could devise; not even though I have occasionally ordered two and three hundred a day to be cut off by various modes of execution. From these circumstances, so notorious has been the insecurity of the roads in Gûjerat, and so much have travellers of every class and description been exposed to inconvenience and danger, that a native of that seat of the muses, Shirauz, on one occasion, on his arrival at Agrah gave vent to his feelings in these four lines: "I have traversed, through the blessing of Him who to none is accountable, roads of which the soil is saturated with human blood. Well may he be said to have obtained a renewal of life, who had escaped a living man from the perils of Gûjerat."*

To conclude my observations on Gûjerat, I shall here add, that the province is altogether a month's journey in compass, the frontiers covered with tracts of forest and woody hills, not to be traversed by man without the greatest difficulty, these being the haunts of wild beasts, and animals of many strange and uncommon varieties. At the period I was about to enter the province from Mandou, on the occasion recently referred to, I directed Nour-ud-dein Kûly Khaun

* There is little doubt that these statements relate to the depredations of the Bheils and Grausssiahs, who long proscribed from the pale of human protection, are by this time, I trust, through the wiser mildness of the British Government, restored to the common benefits of civilized society.

Khaun to furnish himself with what sums of money he might require from the treasury, and through the forest tract on that side prepare a passage for the imperial armies; and that officer, with twenty thousand pioneers, succeeded in a short time, with their saws and hatchets, in cutting a road a bow-shot wide across the whole line of forest, through which we passed with perfect ease and safety.

From Ahmedabad to the sea-coast is a distance of three days' journey; and as I had long wished to view the wonders of the deep, I now proceeded to Khambaït, or Cambay, at the head of the gulf of that name. Here I caused to be constructed on piles, to the distance of a league within the sea, a large stage or pier, which I secured against the impulse of the waves by anchors of a thousand and two thousand maunns' weight. From this, for seven days and as many nights, embarking on board of the ghraubs, or prowed vessels employed on these coasts, I enjoyed in all its perfection the amusement of fishing.

Leaving Cambay and its sea-beaten shore, I directed my course next towards the city of Oujein, one of the most ancient in the whole territory of Hindûstaun. On the banks of a large lake of fresh water near the city, and which washes the foot of the castle walls, I caused on my arrival to be erected, for my accommodation, a pavilion of the largest size, and of the best architecture of the country; and here I remained, hunting and making excursions to various parts of the neighbourhood, for the space of forty days.

While I remained at Oujein on this occasion, an instance of atrocious and sanguinary turpitude occurred, of which the history of crime happily furnishes but few examples.

A certain Moghûl had resided for some time in the place, employed, as was supposed, in the pursuit of some commercial concern; and he was, it seems, in the habit of inviting such females as he observed to be addicted to liquor, to meet him in some of the gardens in the vicinity, where he told them they would find and experience from him such a reception as would surpass their most luxurious expectations.

The women thus invited usually arrayed themselves in their richest ornaments, and thus repaired to the place of appointment; where, as it afterwards appeared, it was the practice of the villain first to reduce them to a state of intoxication, and then to murder and strip them of their ornaments, with which he returned to his own residence. This he was permitted to continue for many a week, until he had by these nefarious means contrived to amass treasure to the amount of five-and-forty thousand tomauns.*

At last one of the women thus invited, after arraying herself, as was his rule

to

* At thirty-three rupees to the tomaun, this would be about fourteen lacs and eighty-five thousand rupees, or about £150,000.

to stipulate, in her richest ornaments, proceeded to the place of assignation accompanied by a groom and female attendant, and, according to appointment, found the Moghûl expecting her arrival. After entertaining the unhappy woman until midnight, he then made her drunk with liquor; and having murdered both the groom and her attendant, returned, and putting a bow-string about her neck, finally strangled her; and having thus consummated his atrocious design, repaired with his blood-stained spoil to his own abode.

His villany, by some means or other, was at last detected, and the diabolical ruffian, together with the body of the woman he had murdered, and the ornaments of which he had stripped her, were brought before me. I ordered the kotewaul, or lieutenant of Kleir, to make search in the house of the murderer, conceiving that something more might be discovered of the property of his unhappy victims. As I suspected, they brought from thence two chests or boxes, which on being opened in my presence, proved to contain not less than seven hundred sets of female ornaments, all of gold, taken from the unfortunates whom he had thus immolated in the gratification of his detestable avarice. As soon as this circumstance was made public, the relatives of the deceased laid claim to and received the property; and I commanded that the perpetrator of this horrible villany should be immediately led to the great plain, where, as an awful example, he was torn piece-meal with red-hot pincers.

From Oujein, I now proceeded on my return towards Agrah, and in due course reached Futtahpour, where I remained for the space of four months, an alarming mortality then prevailing at Agrah. When, however, the mortality ceased, and the air began to be restored to its purity, I quitted Futtahpour, and took up my residence in the Dohrrah gardens, situated in the outskirts of the metropolis. These gardens had been formed by my father in the early part of his reign, and they contain within their precincts four separate pieces of water, each of them a quarter of a farsang, or about a thousand paces, in length and breadth, and each having on its bank a lofty and elegant pavilion. The gardens are, moreover, remarkable for a great many ancient cypress trees of extraordinary size; and it contains also fruit-bearing trees in the greatest number and variety.

Before I quitted these gardens for my final entry into Agrah, I considered it a sacred duty to visit the tomb of my father at Secundera, over which the buildings which I had long since ordered had been now completed, and, in truth, it exhibited to the view in all its parts an object of infinite gratification and delight. In the first place, it was surrounded by an enclosure or colonnade, which afforded standing for eight thousand elephants, and a proportion of horses, the whole being built on arches, and divided into chambers. The principal gate by which you enter is thirty cubits wide, by as many in height, with a tower erected on

four

four lofty arches, terminating in a circular dome, the whole one hundred and twenty cubits high, divided into six stories, and decorated and inlaid with gold and lapis lazuli from roof to basement. This superb portico, as it may be called, has also on each of its four sides (angles probably) a minaret of hewn stone three stories or stages in height. From the entrance to the building in which reposes all that is earthly of my royal father, is a distance of nearly a quarter of a farsang, the approach being under a colonnade floored with red stone finely polished, five cubits wide. On each side of the colonnade is a garden planted with cypresses, wild pine, plane, and sûpaury trees (the betel-nut tree, or arek), in great number; and in the gardens on each side, and at the distance of a bow-shot from each other, are reservoirs of water, from each of which issues a fountain or *jet d'eau*, rising to the height of ten cubits; so that from the grand entrance to within a short distance of the shrine, we pass between twenty of these fountains. Above the tomb itself is erected a pavilion of seven stories, gradually lessening to the top, and the seventh terminating in a dome or cupola; which, together with the other buildings connected with it in every part of the enclosure, is all of polished marble throughout; and all completed, from first to last, at the expense of one hundred and eighty lacs of rupees.* In addition to this I have provided that a supply of two hundred measures or services of food, and two hundred of confectionery, should be daily distributed to the poor from the sacred edifice, and that no strangers should ever be required to dress their own meals, though their number should amount to a thousand horse.

When I entered on this occasion the fabric which enclosed my father's remains, such were my impressions, that I could have affirmed the departed monarch was still alive, and seated on his throne, and that I was come to offer my usual salutation of homage and filial duty. I prostrated myself, however, at the foot of the tomb, and bathed it with the tears of regret and sincerity. On leaving the venerated spot, and in propitiation of the pure spirit which reposed there, I distributed the sum of fifty thousand rupees among the resident poor. I then mounted my horse and proceeded into the castle of Agrah, to the saloon, or palace, which I had ordered to be there built for my own residence.

This pavilion, or rather saloon, rests upon the gate which opens on the river Jumnah, and is supported by twenty-five pillars, all covered with plates of gold, and all over inlaid with rubies, turquoises, and pearl. The roof on the outside is

* About £1,800,000. That the imperial biographer does not here exaggerate, we have the evidence of the lamented and excellent Bishop Heber, who visited the tomb of Akbar, about three kôsse from Agrah, in his journey through upper India during 1824-25. It is also satisfactory to observe, that the British Government has taken this beautiful mausoleum under its protection.

is formed into the shape of a dome, and is also covered with squares of solid gold, the ceiling of the dome within being decorated with the most elaborate figures of the richest materials and most exquisite workmanship. The adjoining tower is a structure of four stories, all decorated in the same costly manner as I have just described, and is from top to bottom of an octagonal shape. Annexed to this latter structure is a small gallery overlooking the Jumnah, from whence, when so disposed, I have been accustomed to view the combats of elephants, neilahgaos, antelopes, and other wild animals. In another story in this building, more on a level with the river, I occasionally distribute to the ameirs of my court, in social communion, wine from my own goblet; and in this same gallery it is that those entitled to particular privileges are admitted to a seat in my presence.

There is, however, another saloon of general audience, to which all classes of the people, high and low, without exception, are admitted to my presence; but in this a recess is parted off by a lattice-work of gold; and at the front of the hall is formed an area, in which is erected a mohidjer (or balustrated stage perhaps) of the height of a man from the ground, also of gold, where the most distinguished members of my court, princes of the blood, and nobility from the rank of one thousand to that of five thousand, are appointed to take their stand on occasions of state and ceremony. The area is covered all over with carpets of thirty and forty cubits, and above is a triple canopy of velvet wrought with gold, as a protection against the rays of a meridian sun. The lattice-work and platform are both of solid gold, and so contrived as to be easily taken to pieces, for removal from place to place, always forming a part of the imperial equipage or equipment, ready to be set up whenever necessary. I shall only add, that the quantity of three thousand maunns of gold* was expended in the fabrication of this article of the imperial appointments.

Having now taken up my abode at Agrah for a permanence, I despatched a message to Allahabad, requiring the presence of my son Sûltan Parveiz, whose head-quarters were at that station. Accordingly, when information reached me that he was arrived within a day's journey of Agrah, I commanded the whole of the ameirs and dignitaries of the empire to quit the city, and proceed to meet him, in order to form his escort to my presence. The instructions of ceremony which I gave them on this occasion were as follows:—when they came within the distance of a bow-shot of the prince and his retinue, they were to dismount from their horses and to salute him on foot, and so continue until they had his permission to remount: but from this an exemption was made in favour of

R Ettamaud-

* At twenty-eight pounds to the maunn only, this would make the trifling quantity of forty-two tons of gold!

Ettamaud-ud-Doulah, who, after paying his respects on foot, was to remount without further ceremony. Thus not much less than twenty thousand of the most distinguished individuals of my court and army were sent to conduct the prince to my presence, with orders to lodge him on the evening of his arrival in the Gûlafshaun garden (the rose-shedding).

On the ensuing day I gave directions, that between the castle of Agrah and the garden where the prince had taken up his residence for the night, and which is at the distance of half a farsang from the castle, there should be stationed at regular intervals twenty nuggarahs or bands of music, to sound the strains of triumph at his approach. At the same time the greater part of the inhabitants of the city, both male and female, in their gayest apparel, proceeded to meet the Shahzadah. Three thousand of my finest elephants, in their richest caparisons of pearl and gold, were drawn out on the road by which he was to approach. Lastly, I sent him a dress of honour from my own wardrobe, with the cincture set with diamonds from my own waist, of the value of four laks of rupees; the diamond jeigha, or aigrette, from my own turban, of the value of one lak, and a chaplet of pearl of the value of five laks of rupees. But this was not all: I intimated that every individual person of my court, of whatever degree, desirous of evincing his attachment to me, each according to his ability, should make a present of some value to the Shahzadah; and by an account subsequently laid before me, it appeared that he received on this occasion, in consequence of such intimation, in gold and jewels, horses and elephants, what amounted in the whole to the value of two hundred laks of rupees.*

In the course of the day they conducted Parveiz across the Jumnah into the castle of Agrah, where he was led immediately into my presence. The moment he came in sight of me, and yet at some distance off, he laid his forehead to the floor, and thus seven times repeated his prostrations until he nearly approached my person. After the seventh he stood erect before me, with his hands crossed upon his bosom. It was now that I directed Saadek Mahommed Khaun and Khojah Abûl Hussun, one of my Bukhshies, to support him, one at each shoulder, up the throne, in order to kiss my feet; and this done, I desired him to take his seat at my right hand, my son Khoorum being on this occasion seated on my left. I then gave orders that the palace of Mohaubet Khaun should be cleared for his reception: that chief being absent at the time, employed in quelling some disturbances on the frontiers of Kabûl, and his family being by my directions removed to another place of residence.

On the day following Parveiz came to pay the ceremonial visit of homage, on which occasion the following enumeration will exhibit a tolerable view of the nature

* Equal to £2,000,000.

nature of the articles which composed his superb present to me. Eighty trained elephants of the highest value; two hundred horses of the best breed of Irâk, with their caparisons wrought in gold; one thousand camels of the dromedary sort, chosen for their speed; a number of the large white oxen of Gûjerat; four hundred trays of gold brocade, velvet, satin, and other pieces of manufacture of the rarest fabric; and twelve trays of jewels, consisting of diamonds, rubies, pearls, and turquoises; altogether, according to the schedule, being equivalent to the magnificent sum of four hundred laks of rupees.* On my part, throwing round his neck a chaplet of pearl of the value of ten laks of rupees, I raised him at once from the order of ten thousand to that of thirty thousand horse.

About a month subsequent to his arrival at Agrah on this occasion, Parveiz surprised me one day, by appearing before me with a napkin fastened round his neck, and casting himself at my feet, breaking out into the bitterest expressions of sorrow. Something astonished, I demanded with paternal solicitude what it was that he would ask—what was the cause of this paroxysm of grief, and what it was that he had to complain of? He replied, that it was beyond his endurance longer to reflect, that himself and his three brothers should be passing their lives in hunting, and in every species of amusement, indulgence, and ease, while one brother, the eldest of all, was condemned now for the fifteenth year to drag on a wretched existence in the solitude of a prison: it was not the lot of humanity to be entirely blameless; but in all circumstances, clemency was the peculiar and most becoming attribute of kings. His humble prayer therefore was, that I would at length grant to this brother my full pardon, release him from his melancholy confinement, and restore him to an exalted place in my royal favour. I found it no easy matter to parry this very urgent supplication, and I therefore demanded if he was prepared to be responsible that the unhappy Khossrou would never again commit himself by the same disloyal and refractory conduct; in which case alone I might, perhaps, be persuaded to set him once more at large. Parveiz immediately committed to paper a few lines, in the nature of a surety bond, and I accordingly signified my assent to the release of Khossrou.

That this might be done with all due formality, I directed a grand entertainment to be prepared in the Dohrrah Bâgh, formerly mentioned; whither on a day appointed I repaired from my palace at Agrah, and from thence I despatched Assof Khaun and Khaun-e-Jahaun with instructions, after giving him some requisite admonition, to bring Khossrou out of his prison. In the mean time I sent him from my own wardrobe a complete dress, with girdle and jeighah set

 with

* £4,000,000, at a moderate computation of two shillings to the rupee.

with diamonds, a horse with enriched caparison, and the elephant Kohpârah, for which my father had paid no less a sum than four laks of rupees, and which had hitherto always belonged to my imperial retinue, with a seat or houdah fitted to its back at the expense of nearly thirty laks of rupees,* equal to ninety thousand tomauns of Irâk.

In order to complete what was requisite to support the splendour of his rank as a prince of the blood, I conveyed to him, moreover, two hundred and three horses of the best breed in the imperial stables, and I directed that the ameirs of every rank that might be disposed to pay him their respects, should not approach him without a suitable present; and all were commanded to attend him on foot, from the place of his confinement to the Dohrrah Bâgh, the distance of a quarter of a farsang, with the exception, as in the case of Sûltan Parveiz, of Ettemaud-ud-Doulah. Such was the display of magnificence and returning royal favour with which, after he had been discarded from my presence for a period of fifteen years,† I admitted Khossrou to do homage to my person.

When he approached the audience-chamber, and appeared in sight at some distance from the throne, he burst into a flood of tears, and repeatedly prostrating himself on the floor, so continued to do until he came close up, when placing his head at my feet, he there remained, without attempting to raise it up, for a full hour, although frequently importuned by me to look up. "With what face," he exclaimed, "can I raise mine eyes to my royal father's countenance? For an offence so heinous as that of which I have been guilty, how can I presume to ask forgiveness?" After shedding a profusion of tears, however, he at last arose, and in some verses expressive of his deep distress, implored my clemency for the past, and my indulgence for the future. Having so far testified his bitter remorse, he again bowed himself to the earth, and then, in an attitude of the utmost humility, standing before me with his hands across his bosom, he repeated, that he could never sufficiently atone or abate his sense of shame for his conduct, though night and day were consumed in endless regret in my presence.

I now ordered a jar of wine, and a goblet inlaid with precious stones, to be brought in, and directing my four sons, Khossrou, Khoorum, Parveiz, and Sheheryaun to seat themselves together, called upon them to circulate the goblet one to the other, while I looked on aloof, to witness this new scene of harmony and reconciliation. My fifth and remaining son, Sûltan Bukht, was at this time absent in Bengal, employed in suppressing the turbulent and disaffected among the

* £300,000. But £40,000 for an elephant must surely be an exaggeration.

† This fixes the date to the sixteenth of the reign of Jahangueir, about A. D. 1621 or 1622.

the natives of that province. The four brothers passed the goblet round accordingly, and in the height of exhilaration began to embrace and kiss each other. However, in conclusion, throwing himself at my feet, Parveiz acknowledged the unspeakable gratification of the moment; but he said there was still one thing wanting to render their happiness complete. He and two of his brothers, he said, were in possession of the several dignities of forty, thirty, and twenty thousand horse, and if a corresponding dignity were bestowed upon their elder brother, every remnant of regret would be effectually removed. The fraternal intreaties of Parveiz finally prevailed, and I granted to Khossrou the patent of an ameir of twenty thousand. In this I could not but consider, that after me the imperial dignity must of right devolve upon Shahzadah Khossrou, it being a maxim in the Teymûrian family, that while the eldest born is living, the monarchy shall never pass to a junior. Under every consideration, I therefore gave him full pardon for his offences, and restored to him all his honours, allowing him the range of ten and twenty days' journey round the metropolis, for his hunting parties and other excursions of amusement. Upon a wholesome male progeny, indeed, rest the sure permanence and stability of sovereign power; and an opposite treatment would have been as inconsistent with sound policy, as it would be unworthy of the authority which I hold.

About the period of which I have been speaking, the design of visiting Kashmeir and its blooming saffron meads took possession of my mind, and I issued orders for the construction of four hundred vessels such as are employed on the Ganges and Jumnah, it being my intention to proceed by water, at least to the foot of the mountains. In the course of two months these were completed, all with awnings and curtains of elegant materials and workmanship. A sum of ten laks of rupees was also advanced to Nour-ud-dein Kûly Beg, for the purpose of being applied to the clearing away the forest thickets, and to the erection of bridges across the rivers, where necessary, to facilitate the passage of the imperial armies.

My residence at Agrah had now continued for several months without interruption, and I had proceeded thence the distance of a day's journey along the river Jumnah upwards, on my way to Dehly, when intelligence was brought to me that the king of the Mugs,* with an army of two hundred thousand men, all of them carrying fire-arms, had landed in Bengal from the seaward, and unexpectedly attacked Kaussem Khaun, who commanded in the province as the lieutenant-general of my son Sûltan Bukht. The report, moreover, added that the enemy had in his fleet of ghraabs a formidable train of heavy artillery, and implements of combustion beyond all calculation; that this formidable arma-

ment

* The natives of Arracan, sometimes so called.

ment had come upon Kaussem Khaun when he was totally unprepared; that his exertions to assemble a fleet and army had been anticipated by this king of the Mugs, by whom he had been surrounded on every side; and that having been severely wounded in four places, he had been defeated with great loss, and finally compelled to abandon his troops to their fate. He had however contrived to throw himself into one of the fortified towns of the province, which he was determined not to surrender to the enemy.

On receipt of this untoward piece of information I directed Mokurreb Khaun, Vezzeir Khaun, and Shujayet Khaun, each of them dignitaries of seven thousand, and each of them victor in a variety of sanguinary conflicts, with sixty thousand veteran Ouzbek horse, which I placed under their orders, three hundred pieces of artillery, and twenty thousand matchlockmen on foot, to proceed immediately to the relief of Kaussem Khaun. The three commanders had my instructions, should the force of the enemy on their arrival in Bengal appear beyond all proportion superior, to apprize me without delay of the fact; and that my son Parveiz should, if necessary, hasten to their support, with one hundred thousand cavalry placed at his disposal.

Before they reached Mauldah, however, the three commanders received intelligence, that having at last assembled the ameirs from every quarter of the province, a circuit of six months' journey in extent, Kaussem Khaun with one hundred thousand horse and foot, all with fire-arms and inured to battle, had attacked the enemy, elated as they were with success, on four sides at once; and that having killed thirty thousand of these ferocious invaders, the rest had taken to flight, eagerly pursued by the conquerors. The latter followed the enemy into their own territories, where they made captive forty thousand boys and girls, the children of the fugitives; and these, together with the heads of the thirty thousand slain, were forwarded to my presence in the course of time. In acknowledgment of this eminent piece of service, I advanced the dignity of Kaussem Khaun by the addition of a thousand horse, conveying to him, at the same time a girdle, sword, and jeighah, set with precious stones, a charger with enriched caparison, and an elephant which had been purchased for my own imperial train at the price of not less than four laks of rupees.* I sent him, moreover, a complete dress taken from my own private wardrobe.

The three detached khauns having proceeded so far to the support of Kaussem Khaun, they were now further directed to enter the country of the Mugs with their united force, and I entertained but little doubt that, with God's grace and the influence of my victorious destiny, the power of the enemy would soon be exterminated

* £40,000 appears an enormous sum to be paid for an elephant; this must, therefore, have been a gross error in the copyist.

exterminated root and branch. Moreover, it was understood that the territory of the Mugs was the resort of great numbers of the very finest elephants, of which as many as could be laid hold of, they were instructed to convey to my presence.

In one month after my departure from Agrah I entered Dehly; and here it was my lot to receive information from Kanouje, that certain of the misguided people in that neighbourhood had raised the standard of rebellion, expelled the officers of my government from several of the purgunnahs or townships in that quarter, and evinced in other respects the most turbulent, refractory, and hostile designs. One of the ablest and bravest men about my court was Abdullah Khaun, and him I now determined to employ, in order to reduce these insolent rebels to their duty. In passing his troops in review before me, it was however observed that he had no elephants suited to the services of a campaign, and I therefore presented him with five of the largest class. I added to these three horses of the breed of Irâk, together with two thousand camels of the fleetest kind, and a donation of ten laks of rupees, all of which to give him a competent equipment, and enable him with the greater confidence to proceed against the insurgents.

We are told by a maxim founded on experience, to beware, when in the season of action you send your generals to the jaws of danger, that you distribute to them liberally the marks of your bounty, in gold and horses, and the other appendages of grandeur, so that nothing may be wanting to encourage them to prosecute the services of the state with vigour and devotion. It happens too frequently that the agents of government shall waste the resources of the districts intrusted to their care in improvident extravagance and luxurious indulgence; and hence it comes to pass, that when the hour of trial arrives they are equally lost to themselves and to their duty. If then at the very crisis of danger I should be induced to withhold my bounty, the manifold evils that must befal the people, whom I may unfortunately have placed at their discretion, in every species of tyranny and misgovernment, would be beyond all endurance; and at the awful day of retribution what a dreadful responsibility would rest upon my shoulders! When therefore emergencies of danger arrive, there is but one alternative—you must disburse your treasure, though it require a houseful of gold.

The next time that Abdullah Khaun passed in review, he communicated the request that his brother might be permitted to join him; considering, as he alleged, should the enemy assail him with a force so superior as to risk some disastrous failure, that the support of so near a relative would be of the utmost consequence. His brother was a commander of the order three thousand, and a request so reasonable could not well be resisted; and the force which was placed

placed at his disposal was thus completed to thirty thousand cavalry of the four-horse class, and ten thousand camel-mounted gunners.

It was not long before Abdullah Khaun found himself in presence of the rebels; who with apparent resolution, and a force little less than one hundred thousand horse and foot, of every description, prepared to give him battle. The advanced parties commenced the action by a discharge of rockets and match-locks; while Abdullah Khaun, having detached his brother to make an attack from an unexpected quarter, with his own division charged the enemy in full career directly in front. Twenty thousand of the rebels fell in this charge; and the remainder taking flight in dismay, crowded into one of their forts (probably that of Kanouje), from the walls and towers of which they opened a fire of artillery and musketry upon their pursuers. Without regarding the briskness of the fire thus kept up by the enemy, Abdullah Khaun with equal gallantry and presence of mind determined to storm the place; and the cavalry emulating the courage of their general, each horseman alternately springing forward, with invincible resolution, to take the place of his comrade as he fell, the principal gateway was at last carried; and ten thousand more of the rebels falling in the defence, their commander fell alive into the hands of the assailants.

The cap, or tiara, of the chief, containing jewels to the value of twenty laks of rupees, and ten thousand of the heads of the rebels, fixed on spears, with all the commanders who were taken alive, were conveyed to my presence, Abdullah Khaun remaining in full possession of the subjugated districts. To deter others from the commission of similar acts of rebellion towards their sovereign, and of ungrateful perfidy towards their benefactor, I directed the bodies of the slain who fell in the defence of Kanouje, to the number of ten thousand, to be suspended from trees with their heads downwards, on the different high roads in the vicinity. And here I am compelled to observe, with whatever regret, that notwithstanding the frequent and sanguinary executions which have been dealt among the people of Hindûstaun, the number of the turbulent and disaffected never seems to diminish; for what with the examples made during the reign of my father, and subsequently of my own, there is scarcely a province in the empire in which, either in battle or by the sword of the executioner, five and six hundred thousand human beings have not, at various periods, fallen victims to this fatal disposition to discontent and turbulence. Ever and anon, in one quarter or another, will some accursed miscreant spring up to unfurl the standard of rebellion; so that in Hindûstaun never has there existed a period of complete repose.

At the period of which I am speaking, I appointed Lushker Khaun to the government of Agrah, and the superintendence of its castles, together with that

that part of my harram left in the metropolis. His son-in-law, Baba Meiret, a brave old man, who had eminently signalized his courage on many occasions, but particularly on the frontiers of Kabul, where he received ten separate wounds, although not before he had contrived to strike off forty of the enemy's heads, was now selected by me to discharge the duties of kotewaul (or prefect of police) of the city of Agrah.

In quitting the metropolis on the present occasion, on board of my flotilla on the Jumnah, I was accompanied by four hundred of the inmates of my harram. Occasionally we came to a spot which furnished game and sport of different kinds, and here I usually disembarked to amuse myself in hunting or shooting; the army which was to accompany us into Kashmeir proceeding all the while on a parallel line, at the distance of three farsangs from the banks of the river.

In our voyage up the Jumnah, when we reached Muttra, which is a celebrated sanctuary of the Hindûs, it was reported to me that there lived in the neighbourhood, where he had resided for twenty years, a noted derweish, or recluse, on whose head, it was stated, there fell every Friday evening throughout the year, from the skies, a shower of gold of coined ashrefies of two methkals each, to the number of five hundred ashrefies. As this was a miracle to which I could not immediately give credit, I determined to ascertain the truth, and for that purpose proceeded to visit the derweish. When I approached the hermitage or cell where he had taken up his abode, I found about four hundred of his disciples clothed in skins, and seated in ranks round the entrance. One of them had previously announced my approach. When I entered the abode of the recluse, which appears to have been a sort of cavern, he did not attempt to move, neither did he offer me the usual salutation, nor the slightest mark of respect in any way whatever. Having, however, made my salaam to him, and otherwise testified my humble respect, I endeavoured by all the mildness I could assume to bring him into conversation. At last he condescended to open his mouth, and his first words were these: "I serve that king who sustains, rambling about the earth, many such kings as thou art." To this observation I replied by a request that he would favour me with something that might remind me of the admonitions of the wise and good. "Strive for the repose of God's creatures committed to thy care," said he, "and do thy pleasure, for the virtue of this will be a cover to thy sins. Be not offensive. In the agents whom thou mayest employ in the different provinces of the empire, be it thy study to reject such as are tyrannical and rapacious. Whilst thou hast power, cherish and respect the grey beard and the derweish." He then recited six lines of poetry of which the following may be the substance: "Scoff not at the aged man weighed down by the hand of affliction; kindle not the flame which consumes the broken-hearted. Be not at one time a trifler, at another grave. Art thou full? give not words of wind. Be not evil-minded lest thy words be evil; be not slanderous if thou wouldst avoid a name of reproach." When he had concluded his recital he said, "let thy treatment of thine eldest son be something better than he has recently experienced, for he is destined to be thy successor."*

In about an hour afterwards the evening closed in upon us, and one of the derweishes in attendance gave the call to prayer. Some tapers were lighted up, and the venerable recluse proceeded to the performance of his devotions, bending his body at intervals eight times to the earth. Immediately afterwards five of the ministering derweishes entered, and stood in an erect posture before their principal. The latter raised his hands towards heaven, and he had scarcely commenced this act of adoration, when all at once a shower of gold from the sky, in laminæ† of about one methkal in weight, fell upon his head, which when collected together amounted in the whole to the value of seven hundred ashrefies. This he divided into two equal parts; one of which he presented to me, with the desire that for a blessing upon my treasury it might be distributed among my officers of revenue; the other he shared among the derweishes present at our conference. Having attentively witnessed all that passed, I did not omit to apprize the recluse, that I should endow his cloister with the assignment of a village producing an annual revenue of fifty thousand rupees, for the subsistence of the devout men who attended upon him. "Apply this money," said he, "to the support of those whose reliance is upon human charity; I need it not, for the things of this life are no longer objects either of care or anxiety to me."‡

Without enlarging further on the subject, I took leave of the recluse; but when I had proceeded a short distance from the cave (or perhaps grotto) in which he resided, the thought occurred to me that I ought to have kissed his hand on departure: and at the very instant the idea was crossing my mind, one of the attendant derweishes came from his principal, with his salutation of peace, to say that he was aware of my thoughts; that he had accepted of the will for the deed, and that it would be inauspicious to return upon my steps after proceeding so far. He had only one further request to make, that for his sake I would extend my particular protection to a certain derweish of his acquaintance, whose

* The derweish proved a false prophet: the elder son, Khossrou, was assassinated by his brother Khoorum, afterwards Shah Jehan.

† Mûtelless is the word in the original: 'flattened pieces or flakes.'

‡ This passage is given in a great measure from conjecture, for the manuscript here, as well as elsewhere in many parts, is written with great negligence and obscurity.

whose abode was at Dehly. Upon this proof of the faculty which he possessed of diving into the minds of man, my faith in his piety was increased an hundred-fold. I turned round on the spot towards the cell of the recluse, and prostrate on the earth, besought the influence of his sacred character, to strengthen my energies for future exertion.

One circumstance more and I shall dismiss this subject altogether. When I returned to the imperial encampment, after quitting the abode of the recluse, it was communicated to me that the son of Khaun-e-Douraun had dared to turn into ridicule my conduct on this occasion. " How childish," said he, " in the emperor, to be magic-blinded by his visit to this canting derweish!" I must here observe, that if I had not received the proof to which I have referred of his power of penetrating into the secrets of the mind, the miracle of the golden shower would have found but little credit with me; but the disrespectful language in which this person presumed to express himself could not be entirely overlooked: I therefore commanded that one side of his head and face should be flayed of the skin, and in that state he was led round the encampment, proclamation being made at the same time that such was the punishment which awaited those who dared to apply disrespectful language to him, who was at once their sovereign and benefactor. My severity on this occasion seemed to be further warranted by the fact, that this same son of Khaun-e-Douraun, on a previous visit to the derweish, had demeaned himself very contemptuously; and the derweish resenting such conduct, ventured to tell him that he should not go so far as to take his head, his youth and rashness being beneath his notice, " but," said he, " I will have thee scalped." And thus was the saying of the derweish pointedly fulfilled. In truth, persons of this description have at all times a claim to our respect; for although devout and pious men possess no claim to be considered as divinities, yet are they not very far apart from the Deity.

At Muttra my son Parveiz separated from the imperial army, and proceeded by my orders to his government of Allahabad. At first, as in the case of others, he had been invested with the order of two thousand, but I had finally advanced him to the commandery of twenty thousand horse: and here I think it no more than strict justice to record, that whether present or absent, never on any occasion have I experienced from him the slightest cause of offence; and I cannot therefore but express my earnest hope, that in all his pursuits he may experience the full attainment of all his wishes. One very trifling exception I may be allowed to introduce. Soon after his departure on this occasion, he conveyed a complaint to me, that having arrived at the distance of two marches

 from

from the camp of Abdullah Khaun above-mentioned, that commander had neglected to pay him that visit of respect, to which as my son he considered himself entitled. I informed him, however, in reply, that in omitting to throw himself in the way for the mere purpose of flattering his vanity, Abdullah Khaun had acted in strict conformity with his allegiance as a dutiful subject: for had he done otherwise, most assuredly he would have been sent to atone for his officiousness and folly by an imprisonment of thirty good years in the castle of Gualiar. Neither can I omit to observe that, however Shahzadah Parveiz may have been offended, there was nothing in the mere gratification of a childish vanity to justify the smallest delay in the march of Abdullah Khaun, whose conduct was governed by the strictest propriety.

While I remained in the precincts of Dehly, at the period to which I shall now return, they described to me a species of feathered game, with tails of a particular description, and the flesh of which was of a flavour in the highest degree delicious. But what more particularly attracted my curiosity was, that they spoke a language known to none but to the natives of Kashmeir, who, by using a sort of note or call, took from them the power of flight; and who were thus able to catch them by thousands at a time. On a plain in the neighbourhood, frequented by thousands of these birds in a flock, by way of experiment, I employed about a thousand of the Kashmeirians accustomed to the business, to give me a proof of their skill, and I attended in person to view the sport. As had been represented to me, about twenty of the Kashmeirians collected together, and produced a sort of murmuring sound, which attracting the attention of these birds, they were drawn by degrees within such a distance of the men, that they were taken in entire flocks. My pity was greatly moved by the reflection that these harmless birds should have fallen victims to this sort of treachery; that they should have been betrayed into the hands of the destroyer by their irresistible love of harmonious sounds, and that I should be found capable of consigning them to slaughter from a mere idle and vicious curiosity; the next day, therefore, I caused the whole, to the number of twenty thousand birds which had been taken on the occasion, to be set at liberty. My object was obtained in witnessing the fact, but to have seen them slaughtered would have bespoken a want of compassion foreign to my nature.

On my arrival at Sehrind, I visited the gardens of Khojah Weissy, constructed some time before by my directions. This person, distinguished not less for his skill in architecture than for his taste in laying out gardens and ornamental grounds, had indeed, in the present instance, exercised his judgment with such complete success, as to afford me the utmost delight. In particular I must describe, that

that on entering the garden I found myself immediately in a covered avenue, planted on each side with scarlet roses, and beyond them arose groves of cypress, fir, plane, and evergreens, variously disposed; but, what is scarcely credible, all this had been completed in the short space of forty days. Passing through these, we entered what was in reality the garden, which now exhibited a variegated parterre, ornamented with flowers of the utmost brilliancy of colours, and of the choicest kind. In the midst of this open parterre was a noble basin or reservoir of water, and in the centre of this piece of water was an elegant and lofty pavilion, of eight sides, capable of accommodating two hundred persons with convenient sitting-room, and surrounded by a beautiful colonnade. It was, moreover, two stories high, and painted all over within with every description of figure delightful to the eye. The reservoir was faced all round with hewn stone, and nearly two thousand water-fowl sported on its bosom. The infinite variety of flowers and flowering shrubs which bloomed on the parterre was not less delightful to the sight than bewitching to the smell: and as some acknowledgment of the gratification which I had experienced, I raised the same Khojah Weissy, on the spot, from the order of seven hundred to that of one thousand horse.

The day after my visit to these gardens, a circumstance occurred which I cannot pass without notice. It was stated to me that the collector of Sehrind had in his hands a petition which he was anxious to present to me, and I directed that he might be immediately sent for. The petition expressed that this collector did not entertain the design of interfering in any way with the property of the Moslems; on the contrary, his object was confined to the fixing of a fair and equitable assessment upon the wealth of the opulent Hindûs. For this purpose, if I could be prevailed upon to issue an ordinance in conformity with his views, he would engage to make good to the imperial treasury the zekkaut of the empire, such as it was in the time of my father Akbar, to the amount of three maunns of gold a day; and, moreover, that he would pay in advance the assessment of three whole years, amounting to not less than thirteeen hundred maunns of gold.* When I had heard with attention what he had further to say on the subject, I desired him to go and bring me the money, in order that I might bestow upon him the employment for which he seemed disposed to make such enormous sacrifice. The collector, who was known to be among the most opulent of the inhabitants

* One lunar year's assessment, at three hundred maunns a day, would be 1,062 maunns; and an assessment of three years would amount to 3,186 maunns of gold, or about forty-four tons and six hundred-weight. Three hundred camels, with a load of three hundred each, would bring forty-five tons, which at sixty-three guineas to the pound-weight of gold, would be equal to 5,670,000 guineas.

inhabitants of Sehrind, quitted my presence accordingly; and shortly afterwards re-appeared, bringing with him the whole of the gold, loaded on five hundred camels, each load in wrappers of the finest scarlet of Irâk. I ordered ten of the loads to be indiscriminately distributed among those who were present, and the remainder to be lodged in the treasury; after which I desired him to withdraw for the present, and to appear before me again on the ensuing morning, when the patent of his appointment would be delivered to him.

The next morning, before the sun was well up, the collector, arrayed in his gayest apparel, with a chaplet of pearl about his neck of the value of a lak of rupees, and his bosom full of hope and expectation, came to do homage for his appointment. I requested to know whether the whole of the gold which he had placed at my disposal, as the purchase of his office, was exclusively his own property, or whether it belonged in part to other Hindûs, who would have a share in the profits of his employment. He explained to me in answer, that while in the agonies of death, his father had disclosed to him that in a certain secret place under ground he had concealed in large jars a mass of treasure, which in the hour of distress he might employ to relieve himself. "Sire," said he, "than what I have paid into your highness's treasury for my appointment, there is still left in the subterranean more than double the quantity, and there was therefore not the smallest necessity for bringing discredit on my name by borrowing." I could scarcely believe what I heard, and I bluntly told him that I thought he had advanced a falsehood; but if what he said was really true, he could have no objection to point out the spot where this treasure was concealed to Saadek Mahommed Khaun, one of my bukhshies. Without a moment's hesitation he conducted Saadek Mahommed to the place where this enormous treasure lay in deposit; and having so done, both returned to my presence. I considered that I was warranted in retaining for my own use what he had voluntarily placed at my disposal; but it would have been an act of unjust violence if I had taken possession of that which remained in the excavation beneath his house, to the manifest injury of his children.

In these circumstances, I ordered a camel to be brought to my presence, and sending for Nour-ud-dein Kûly, I told him that the dress of the Hindû, with the valuable chaplet of pearl which encircled his neck, was all his own. But he was to conduct the unhappy man to the outside of the town, where he was to cause his bowels to be cut open, after which he was to be fastened to the side of the camel, and so carried round the camp, while a proclamation was made to the following purpose: "Such is the punishment to which that man is doomed, who when his sovereign, from a paternal regard to the welfare of his people for a period of fourteen

fourteen years past, has remitted the impost of the zekkaut, dared to insinuate the advantage of renewing such a tax, and thus bringing upon the benefactor of his people afresh the odium of being their oppressor. Let this be an example to deter the evil counsellor from communicating the slightest hint to give the thoughts of the sovereign a direction so replete with evil to the subject and dishonour to himself.*

It must indeed be considered fortunate, that in this age few men can be found so sordid in principle and expectation, as from the prospect of advantage to themselves, to implicate the sovereign under such a load of guilt and responsibility, from whom alone, on the awful day of reckoning, the account will be required. And what, in gold or jewels, or property of any description, have I lost, that I should venture to reimburse myself in the earnings of the abstinent and industrious merchant—earnings accumulated through a thousand risks, and by so many distant and toilsome journies? An act of such crying injustice could the everlasting God suffer to pass unpunished? "Leaving the issue to God," says the maxim, "be thou the shepherd of his people." There are two faculties of which the Macedonian himself was scarcely master:—"Discard the absurdities of human vanity; this is the ark of knowledge.—Study the knowledge of thy kind; not the patchwork mantle of the devotee.—In a life so transient, suffer not thine exertions to sleep.—Let thy time be so devoted, as to insure the approbation of thy Maker.—Humanity is the essential science, united with valour and beneficence.—If thou hast not these, thou art no more than a statue in the shape of a man.—Thou hast not put in practice the hundredth part of the dictates of science.—If in the study of philosophy thou hast neglected the duties of thy kind, thou art nothing better than a barren branch.—With much labour and exertion only can a man arrive at distinction.—How canst thou obtain the palm of virtue, if thou art the slave of sensuality.—If thou art desirous of the elixir of eternal happiness, know thine own merit; this is the true red sulphur—the powder of transmutation."

When I had passed a week in every species of enjoyment in these gardens, I sent for Khojah Weissy, and with one of my own dresses presented him with thirty thousand rupees in money. I then quitted Sehrind, and proceeded on my way towards Kashmeir, the saffron meads of which I so ardently longed to visit. Having arrived within three days' journey of the city of Lahour, my son Khoorum communicated a request, that he might be allowed an absence of ten days, for the purpose of visiting that noble city, a period of two years having elapsed since

* As the exemption from zekkaut took place either at or soon after the accession of Jahangueir, the excursion to Kashmeir is clearly fixed to the fourteeth year of his reign.

since he last saw the place, and he was desirous of embracing the opportunity to view the progress of the new gardens, buildings, and other improvements which I had ordered for its embellishment. He engaged at the same time to rejoin me on the march before I should have entered the mountain passes.

As I could have no objection to grant such a request, and I was desirous that his visit should be conducted with sufficient splendor, the prince was directed to take with him two hundred camels loaded with enriched caparisons, girdles, kreisses, swords, and head-pieces, minns,* and amberstands, and a variety of other articles, all enriched with pearl and precious stones; all of which, on his arrival within a certain distance of the city, he was to deliver to the kotewaul, or civil governor of the place, together with as much as loaded a thousand camels more in cloth of gold of Khorassaun, velvets from Gûjerat and Kashaun, and piece-goods of the most delicate fabric, all taken immediately from my own equipment stores. The inhabitants of Lahour were directed to afford every assistance towards rendering the reception of the prince on this occasion as magnificent as possible, by decorating the streets and bazars with gold woven carpets, figured draperies or tapestry, both European and Chinese, and canopies also of cloth of gold, both within and without the city, to the distance of nearly four kôsse. All this the kotewaul was to keep in readiness for the space of four or five days.

From Allumgunje, which is at the entrance of Lahour, and where Sûltan Khoorum was to mount his elephant, he was to be preceded by three thousand elephants of his own train, all arrayed in trappings of gold and velvet empowdered with pearl, the gold alone on each elephant being of the weight of five maunns of Hindûstaun; next were fifteen hundred horses of the breed of Arabia, Irâk, and Badakhshaun, all in similar rich and sumptuous caparisons, and each led by a separate groom. Behind the prince were to follow forty elephants bearing the nuggaurah khaunah, or band of kettle-drums, and immediately before him were to be eighty horns and fifty trumpets, rending the air with the din of martial music; the whole being closed by a column of twenty thousand horse, clad in quilted mail, with silken tassels at the end of their lances, and all their horses with ornamental breast-pieces, housings of panther and tyger skins, and tails of the sea-cow suspended to their necks; and in this splendid array was to be the procession through the streets and market-places of the city. The whole of the way by which the dûltaor passed accordingly, for the distance of four kôsse, from bags of money deposited in the howdah of the elephant on which he rode, he continued to scatter, every now and then, on each side of him, handsful of

* Tchaur ayenah, perhaps glass lanterns.

of gold and silver ashrefies and rupees among the people, to the amount of ten laks of rupees in silver, equivalent to thirty thousand tomauns of Irâk, and of two laks of ashrefies of five methkels, equal to one hundred thousand tomauns in gold.*

In this splendid array it was that Shahzadah Khoorum proceeded to the banks of the Rauvy, where a superb display of tents had been set up for his reception; and there he remained for the space of three days, distributing to the minstrels, the sons of song and music, and others who repaired to visit him, and to all according to merit, the most liberal marks of his bounty. On the fourth day he quitted Lahour, in order to return to my presence.

From Lahour to Hussun Abdal, where I lay encamped to await his return, is a distance of five ordinary days' journey.† This, by stationing relays of fresh horses, he performed in one day and a night, thus presenting himself to me within the ten days' absence which he had obtained for his excursion. On this occasion, when he had performed his kornesh (or salutation of homage) before me, his present consisted of jewels to the value of twenty laks of rupees, with three hundred horses of Arabia and Irâk, one thousand despatch camels, and five of the noblest class of elephants, each of the value of three laks of rupees. In return, I raised him from the order of forty thousand, of which he was already in possession, to that of forty-five thousand. I remained at Hussun Abdal for a week, during which, at an entertainment, I presented Shahzadah Khoorum with a chaplet of pearl, which had cost in the purchase the sum of eight and forty laks of rupees.‡

When I gave orders for the march from Hussun Abdal a heavy fall of rain occurred, which continued without intermission for three days and three nights; at the termination of which the rain ceasing, we proceeded to Kalanour, where, however, the river was so greatly swelled by the rain, that the passage of the imperial troops was found impracticable. The next day I gave orders that all classes on their arrival should remain stationary until the flood in the river should abate, when they might proceed to cross without hazard. Nevertheless, all who were in possession of the largest sized elephants ventured to pass their people

T and

* If this statement be correct, two laks of ashrefies would be equal to Rupees 3,333,333⅓, the half of which being rupees 1,666,666⅔, would give something more than sixteen rupees to the ashrefy. I had been told in India, that the ashrefy and the gold mohr were the same thing.

† Hussun Abdal is a considerable distance to the west of Kalanour, and the Emperor must have gone far out of his way, and then returned to the latter place, which is more in the direct road to the pass of Bember.

‡ Nearly half a million sterling.

and baggage to the opposite side; and others, who possessed horses of sufficient strength and activity, cast themselves into the stream without reflection.

Thus it was that the son of Mirza Rûstum, a little boy scarcely out of his childhood, mistaking the ford, cast himself, with ten of his attendants on horseback, into the river, where the water was two spears length deep, and the current so impetuous as to overthrow the strongest elephants. In the middle of the stream the boy was thrown from his horse, and carried away by the torrent; and although every exertion was made by his attendants to rescue him from his watery grave, all was in vain, the poor child perished irrecoverably. The young Mirza had not the slightest knowledge of swimming; but even though he had possessed the greatest skill in the exercise, the force of the stream was such that it would have been unavailing. The ten men who endeavoured to save him also perished.

When the melancholy circumstance was made known to me, I can scarcely describe how deeply I became affected by it. The whole of that night I neither ate, nor drank, nor slept; for my regard for the poor child surpassed all ordinary measure of kindness. Most commonly, when I mounted my elephant, he was my companion, and, seated before me with the keeper's hook in his hand, usually guided the animal in his course. He was, indeed, endowed in every respect with a capacity far beyond his years. A period of six months only had elapsed, since I had married him to a daughter of Ettemaud-ud-Doulah,* with a marriage portion, amounting, in different articles, to the value of twenty laks of five methkaly ashrefies.† He seemed, in every respect, the reverse of his father, brother, and other relatives; and I had recently adopted him as a child of my own. In the severest terms I could express, I reproached his improvident father, for having suffered the child to enter the river on horseback; for which there did not appear the slightest apology, since he had an equipment of fifty or a hundred elephants in his own train. But there seemed to exist some fatal necessity that demanded a victim to be sacrificed of such surpassing purity and excellence. Doubtless this poor child might be justly said to be a second Joseph. Never have I mourned so deeply for the death of any one, as for that of the son of Mirza Rûstum. The following lines may furnish some faint idea of what I endured on the occasion:

"Deprived

* A half-sister, probably, of Nour Jahaun.

† At nine rupees to the ashrefy, this would be one krour and eighty laks of rupees; at fifteen rupees to the same, it would amount to three krour of rupees, or three millions sterling. I have not been able finally to determine which of these valuations is to be assigned to the ashrefy. The name would be exactly rendered in English by the word *noble;* a name not unknown to the English mint.

" Deprived of the roses of thy countenance, how deep, alas, the anguish of my soul!—Thy cruel loss has planted a thousand thorns in my bosom! Whilst thou wert present, the cheerful earth was like a garden of tulips; but the wounds of separation have transferred to my heart the blood-drop tints of that flower. For ever hidden from mine eyes is the dimple of that cheek: those eyes, the lustre of which has been so sadly dimmed with tears. How has the happiness which I enjoyed in thy society been changed to sorrow and sleepless anguish! Torn as thou hast been from my presence, whom have I left to share in my thoughts! Alas! none but the silent tear which lodges in my bosom. Directed by the hand of Destiny, the death-shaft has transfixed thee; but the wound inflicted by the same hath not left me unharmed. What rose in the garden was so blooming as thyself? Alas, that the death-blow should have so early scattered its leaves!—Far more dearly cherished than Joseph by his father; alas, that thou shouldest have thus early become the prey of the all-devouring monster! For the beauty that beamed on thy brows, an hundred and an hundred times, alas!—for thy kind and gentle manners, a thousand times, alas! The spring is come—in the garden buds the rose: to me, alas! the spring has only brought the plant of sorrow—the tree of mourning. The image of thy perfections is for ever stamped within my breast; the lustre of thy beauty will never be lost to mine eyes. Thy life was only budding from the germ; alas! that it should have been so prematurely blighted by the hand of death!—Alas, for thy love, thou star of the meridian of affection!—Alas, for thy blooming youth, thou cypress with the cheek of the rose!—Alas, that the narcissus in thine eye should have been so early quenched in death; that thy glowing cheek should have been so unseasonably lost in the clouds of everlasting night!"*

Without enlarging further on a subject to me so painful, I sent nearly a thousand of the best swimmers into the river, in the hope of recovering the lifeless body of the young Mirza, in order to give it the last mournful proofs of my affection; but all search proved in vain. What became of his poor remains was never discovered. But this is not all that I have to record of this fatal river. Impatient of restraint, the unreflecting multitude plunged in heedless throngs into the stream, and perished to the number of fifty thousand persons, not having the common sense to wait until the waters should have subsided. The cold on the banks of the river was, moreover, so severe, that it was reported to me

* These lines within the inverted commas might be safely omitted without embarrassing the subject; because, though pathetic enough in the original, they have rather a grotesque character in English.

me the next morning that nearly ten thousand elephants, camels, and horses, had perished during the night, belonging to the imperial stables alone, independently of what belonged to the army in general. Blessed be God, for the greatest heats of the dry season! for never, in the very hottest temperature, was there an instance of such extensive destruction at one time. The oldest and most experienced men present united in declaring, that in all they had seen at different times, and in every variety of season, it did not occur to them ever to have witnessed such severity of cold as that which this year had proved so destructive, on hill and plain, to so many animals of every description.

At the foot of the mountains of Kashmeir the snow fell without intermission for seven days and seven nights, and fuel of any description was not to be procured. The army was accompanied by fakeirs, or religious mendicants, in extraordinary numbers, and as they must have perished if not preserved by some immediate intervention, I ordered a lak of camels belonging to the imperial equipment to be employed forthwith in conveying such fuel as could be procured at a distance, to camp, and these fakeirs to be supplied from the very first convoy, otherwise their destruction would have been inevitable. I further directed that each mendicant should be furnished on the occasion with a vest stuffed with cotton, and a sheep-skin cloak.

As soon as the snowy weather had abated, I gave permission to such of the dignitaries and private stipendiaries as were so inclined, to return to Lahour; for it suited but little with my views to expose my people on any occasion to unrequired hardship. Then with such of my store department and artificers, and three hundred of those who usually attended my person, and who indeed were never separated from me, I continued my journey toward Kashmeir, the cold abating in a considerable degree as soon as we had passed the mountain frontier. There, among its saffron plains, I proceeded to amuse myself in hunting and shooting, and in excursions to different parts of this delightful valley, for the period of a month, at the expiration of which I adopted the resolution of returning to Lahour, which I was desirous of revisiting on my way to the metropolis. Seven years had now elapsed since I last left that city; and I had then given orders to throw down the principal towers, and to rebuild them of red hewn stone, in great part sculptured with the figures of different animals. I had moreover directed a four-walled garden to be completed on the banks of the Rauvy, in the neighbourhood of the town.

When I had, however, proceeded a day's journey from Kashmeir, intelligence arrived from Kabûl, stating that the turbulent and factious natives of that province had again thrown off restraint, and were beginning to infest the road, and

and to commit every species of enormity against their fellow subjects. Upon this I directed Mohaubet Khaun, a mûnsebdaur (or dignitary) of my court of the order of five thousand, to proceed immediately to that quarter, with twenty thousand horse of various descriptions, ten thousand camel-mounted matchlockmen, and two hundred elephants of the fiercest class. The origin of this mischief was Allahdaud Khaun, formerly mentioned, a personage of the first distinction among the Afghan tribes, who had withdrawn from my court without the slightest cause, and had now made his appearance in the neighbourhood of Kabûl. My instructions to Mohaubet Khaun, therefore, were, in the event of his being able to lay hold of this person, to send him at all hazard alive to court, in order that he might receive in my very presence the chastisement due to his ingratitude, and thus furnish to the world an example that none would be permitted with impunity to abscond from my presence on every vague and frivolous pretence.

Thus abruptly terminates the Imperial auto-biographer's Memoirs.